Shipping of the Bosphorus
by
Chris Brooks and Simon Smith

We start our photographic journey outside the Bosphorus in the Sea of Marmara. To the east of Istanbul is the harbour of Tuzla. This harbour is a major centre for ship repair as well as shipbuilding, with a large number of repair and construction yards crowded into the semi-circular Aydinli Bay. The large bulk carrier **Angelo Della Gatta** was photographed at a repair yard in Tuzla on 2 June 2008. She had arrived on 10 May 2008 from Taranto and departed on 8 July 2008 for the same port. The **Angelo Della Gatta** was built in 1982 at the Hyundai Heavy Industries yard in Ulsan, South Korea, as the **Pacific Challenge** for the C.Y. Tung Group under the British flag. She carried this name only until 1986 when she took the flag of Panama and her name was changed to **Iron Master**. In 1998 she was sold to Deiulemar Cia di Nav SpA of Italy and became **St. John**

flying the flag of the Bahamas. The same company owned her when she was seen in Tuzla, having renamed her **Angelo Della Gatta** in October 2001. When renamed in 2001 she reverted to the British flag, until 2005 when it changed to that of Italy. Since mid-2006 her trading pattern had been mainly between Point Central, Mauritania and Taranto. Behind the **Angelo Della Gatta** can be seen the Panamanian bulk woodchip carrier **Global Oji** in dry-dock. She was built in 1998 at the Hitachi Shipyard at Maizuru, Japan and is currently operated by the NYK Group. **Global Oji** had arrived at Tuzla on 26 May 2008 from Santander. She departed on 14 June 2008, for Aratu, Brazil. In July 2009 she was renamed **Global Nature** without a change of ownership.

(Chris Brooks)

INTRODUCTION

The Bosphorus, or Bosporus, is the narrow stretch of water that separates the European and Asian parts of Turkey. It is also sometimes referred to as the Istanbul Strait or Istanbul Bogazı. It links the Black Sea, in the North, with the Sea of Marmara, in the South. Another narrow strait of water, the Dardanelles, further separates the Sea of Marmara from the Aegean and Mediterranean seas. The Bosphorus is approximately 32 kilometres in length and varies in width from 3.7 kilometres at its northernmost extremity, where it meets the Black Sea, to 700 metres at its narrowest point between Kandilli and Asiyan. For centuries the Bosphorus has been an important trade route between the Black Sea and the Mediterranean. The Roman emperor Constantine the Great realised the great strategic importance of the area, and founded the city of Constantinople, on the banks of the Bosphorus as his capital of the eastern Roman Empire. In the mid 15th century the Ottoman Empire conquered the area. The region was under Ottoman control until Mustafa Kemal Atatürk, the hero of Gallipoli and the Turkish War of Independence, in the early 1920s, rose to power and subsequently abolished the Ottoman Empire. The new Turkish republic was formed on 29 October 1923. After the First World War the Bosphorus was declared an international territory to enable the free passage of shipping between the Black Sea and Mediterranean. This was amended by the Montreaux Convention in 1936, which allowed the area to revert to Turkish territory, but still permitted shipping free passage through the straits. The area was subsequently remilitarised, and these days, although it is an international shipping lane, Turkey retains the right to restrict naval vessels belonging to non-Black Sea nations sailing through the straits.

The Bosphorus continues to be a vitally important trade route. All shipping from the Black Sea passes through the straits to reach the Aegean and Mediterranean seas and thus the rest of the world. The Black Sea affords the only coastline for several otherwise landlocked countries such as Bulgaria, Romania, Ukraine and Georgia. In addition, the Black Sea coastline of Russia is vitally important to the export of Russian oil reserves to the rest of the world. From the Black Sea it is possible to navigate to the Caspian Sea, through the River Don and River Volga. This further allows access to the coastlines of Azerbaijan, Iran, Kazakhstan and Turkmenistan.

Constantinople is, of course, now known as Istanbul, a city which although not the administrative capital of Turkey is certainly its economic capital. It is a sprawling city estimated to be the home of well in excess of 12 million inhabitants, encompassing both shores of the Bosphorus. The Asian and European sides are connected by two suspension bridges, the southernmost being the Bosphorus Bridge, opened in 1973. The Fatih Sultan Mehmet Bridge, about five kilometres to the north of the first bridge, was opened in 1988. There are plans for a third bridge to the north of the existing two bridges. Numerous ferries connect the European and Asian shores. On the European side the main ferry terminus near the Galata Bridge is at Eminönü. Ferries from here cross to Üsküdar, Haydarpasa and Kadıköy on the Asian side. A new rail tunnel under the Bosphorus will connect the Sirkeci area to the Asian shore. The tunnel, known as the Marmaray, is scheduled to begin operation in 2012.

Since the construction work started on the tunnel several years ago, shipping in the Bosphorus has been restricted to a single southbound or northbound convoy system. Under normal operation, the southbound convoy starts at midday and lasts for 12 hours. The northbound convoy starts at midnight and continues until midday. In practice the changeover times for the convoys can vary according to the number of vessels waiting to transit the strait. The Bosphorus is a very busy waterway with several sharp turns and strong currents. On average there are over 130 vessels transiting the Bosphorus daily. The taking of pilots for vessels passing through the Bosphorus is not compulsory, but recommended for vessels exceeding 150 metres in length. Pilotage through the Bosphorus is, however, compulsory for vessels calling at or having sailed from Turkish ports in the Sea of Marmara. There are certain restrictions affecting large tankers with an overall length in excess of 250 metres transiting the Bosphorus, depending on the time of day and also the weather and sea conditions. Vessels of this size are restricted to a daylight passage and under certain circumstances, a tug escort is required, particularly when tankers are in a loaded condition. Vessels of the former Communist controlled countries of Bulgaria, Romania, Ukraine and Georgia are commonplace as well as Russian vessels trading to the Black Sea coast of that country.

General cargo vessels of the type rarely seen these days in western Europe are still regular visitors to the Bosphorus. Although containerships are relatively common in the area, they are in the minority (less than 10% of the total transits in the Bosphorus). Large tankers transit the Bosphorus regularly, with oil exports from the Russian ports such as Novorossiysk being a major source of tanker traffic.

Since first visiting Istanbul in 2002 as part of a tour organised by the Thames Ship Society, we have paid several return visits. Istanbul and the Bosphorus provides many vantage points and opportunities to photograph and observe large numbers of vessels of all types at close quarters and underway. The purpose of this book is to give the reader an overall view of shipping in the area. It is not intended as a comprehensive guide to the region, nor an in-depth study of shipping. Vessel histories, ownership in particular, are not intended to be comprehensive but we have attempted to highlight facts that may be of interest to the reader. Many hours of research have been spent in the preparation of this book, but, we cannot guarantee that it will be totally error free – for any errors that remain we apologise in advance.

The book is organised on a geographic basis, starting at the southern extremities of the Bosphorus, looking at vessels in the nearby harbour of Tuzla and its shipyards and anchorage. Moving on westwards from Tuzla is Pendik Harbour and the anchorage at Kartal. A large number of vessels can usually be found in this anchorage, either waiting for their next voyage, laid up or awaiting a berth at the nearby Tuzla shipyards.

Next we visit Istanbul anchorage, another busy area where vessels awaiting a transit through the Bosphorus can be found. This anchorage is situated to the south of the European centre of Istanbul. Before proceeding northwards through the Bosphorus we will visit Haydarpasa Harbour, situated on the Asian side of the Bosphorus. We will also view vessels at Istanbul cruise terminal, on the European side of the Bosphorus.

Our journey northbound through the Bosphorus visits several locations where passing shipping can be photographed. Locations include Kandilli and Kanlica on the Asian side of the waterway. On the European shore we visit Rumeli Hisari and Rumeli Kavagi.

Acknowledgements

Many thanks are due to the committee of the Thames Ship Society for introducing us to the delights of Istanbul on our first visit there in 2002. Thanks also to our many friends at home and in Istanbul who have arranged boats for us to get close up views of the vessels in the anchorages and showed us vantage points from which to take photographs. In particular thanks are due to Mehmet Yapici from Foto-IO in Istanbul. Most of all our thanks go to the wonderful city of Istanbul. We much appreciate Bernard McCall for agreeing to take on this project and for producing the high quality finished publication. Grateful thanks also to the staff of the Amadeus Press for their contribution to the finished book.

Chris Brooks & Simon Smith   August 2011

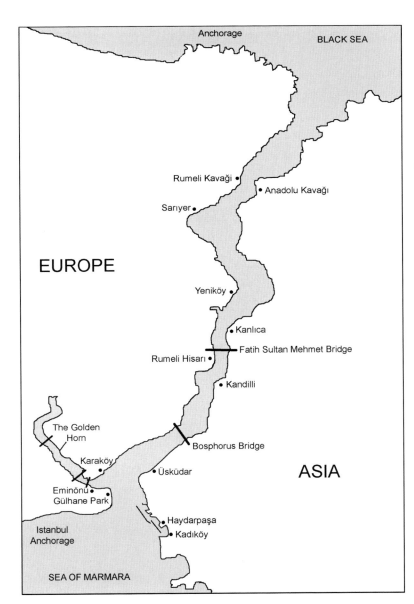

Sources Used

Comecon Merchant Ships	Ambrose Greenway
Jane's Merchant Ships	Jane's
Lloyd's Marine Intelligence Unit	
Lloyd's Register of Shipping	
Lloyd's Shipping Index	
Marine News	World Ship Society
Miramar Ship Index	Roger Haworth
Reefer Ships	Nick Tollerton
SD14 The Full Story	John Lingwood
Soviet Merchant Ships	Ambrose Greenway

Published by Bernard McCall, 400 Nore Road, Portishead, Bristol, BS20 8EZ, England.
Website : www.coastalshipping.co.uk
Telephone/fax : 01275 846178. E-mail : bernard@coastalshipping.co.uk
All distribution enquiries should be addressed to the publisher.

Printed by Amadeus Press, Ezra House, West 26 Business Park, Cleckheaton, West Yorkshire, BD19 4TQ
Telephone : 01274 863210; fax : 01274 863211; e-mail : info@amadeuspress.co.uk; website : www.amadeuspress.co.uk

ISBN : 978-1-902953-53-3

Front cover: The refrigerated cargo ship **Baltic Wave** commences her southbound Bosphorus transit on 30 May 2008. Managed by Baltic Reefers she had sailed from Constantza the previous day and was bound for the Ecuadorian port of Guayaquil via Gibraltar and the Panama Canal. **Baltic Wave** was launched at Smith's Dock Middlesbrough (yard number 1331) in 1976 as **Almeda Star**, one of five "A-class" reefers built for interests managed by Blue Star Line. A sixth of the type was ordered from the Nakskov Shipyard in Denmark. She was renamed **Arran** briefly in 1984 before becoming **Harlech** later that year. Then she reverted to **Almeda Star** in 1988. Following sale to St. Petersburg-based Baltic Reefers in 2001 she became **Baltic Wave**. Her career ended on the beach at Alang in August 2010.

(Simon Smith)

Back cover: The **Sehit Metin Sülüs** is typical of the Bosphorus ferries built locally in Istanbul in the 1980s. She is seen here outward bound from Eminönü during the early evening of 6 June 2008 at the end of another busy rush hour. **Sehit Metin Sülüs** was completed in 1986 by the Türkiye Gemi Sanayii shipyard at Haliç in the Golden Horn, a mere stone's throw from where she was photographed. She carried the name **Metin Sülüs** until 1993 when the prefix Sehit (a Turkish word meaning "martyr") was added.

(Chris Brooks)

We begin at Tuzla. As well as ship repair facilities, Tuzla is also a major shipbuilding area. The various yards specialise in the construction of chemical and product tankers, containerships and tugs. Here we see the launch of the chemical tanker **Besiktas Nordland** from the Gisan Gemi Insa Sanayi shipyard in Tuzla. She was launched on 9 July 2007 as **Besiktas Nordland** and managed by Besiktas Likid Tasımacılık, under the Turkish flag. She was renamed **Selandia Swan** in November 2007, several months before she was completed. At that time her management was taken over by Uni-Tankers A/S of Middelfart, Denmark, flying the Danish International flag. Her initial voyage on completion was into the Black Sea, to the Ukrainian port of Illichivsk, to load a cargo of sunflower oil. On her way from Illichivsk, through the Bosphorus, bound for Dunkirk, she suffered an engine failure on 17 March 2008, which caused the Bosphorus to be closed to traffic for several hours. Once repairs were completed, she headed for Dunkirk. Her main areas of operation are now Scandinavia, the Baltic, western Europe and the western Mediterranean.

(Chris Brooks)

The Meridian type freighter **Blue Lady** lies inactive at Tuzla shipyard on 12 August 2009, having arrived almost six months earlier. Between 1972 and 1981 the Warnowwerft shipyard at Warnemünde, in what was then East Germany, produced 29 of the class. By the end of the millennium nearly half the class had been either delivered to breakers or become total losses. At the end of 2010, only two vessels were believed to remain. She was delivered to the Yugoslav company Jugoslavenska Oceanska Plovidba (Jugooceanija) as **Risan** in October 1981. She continued to operate for Jugooceanija until 1999 when her sale to Panamanian flag interests saw her change name to **Tirisa**. Further sales took place in 2001 and 2005 resulting in name changes to **Splendour** for Panamanian interests and **Lady Flora** for Syrian operator Mamari Shipping Co. In July 2008 she took her current name and was registered under the Turkish flag. She finally left Tuzla in February 2010 arriving off Chittagong in May 2010, following a reported sale to Bangladeshi breakers. A reprieve followed with a change of name to **Destiny**. At the end of 2010 she continues to trade under the St Kitts & Nevis flag for London-based CB Marine Ltd.

(Simon Smith)

The chemical tanker *Caroline Essberger* is seen at Tuzla shipyard on 12 August 2009. She was launched at the Eregli Shipyard, located on Turkey's Black Sea coast, on 30 May 2009. The Eregli yard specializes in chemical tankers and tugs and the order book includes a further three 5,300 deadweight chemical tankers for Essberger Tankers. Shortly after being photographed at Tuzla *Caroline Essberger* joined the fleet of Essberger Tankers sailing under the Dutch flag and registered in Dordrecht. After passing the Dardanelles on 30 August she called briefly at Gibraltar and Huelva before arriving at Antwerp in mid-September. The vessel is named after Caroline von Rantzau, daughter of the parent company's chairman and joint owner. John T Essberger was a German naval commander who founded a shipping company in Hamburg in 1924. In 2004 the Essberger Group acquired the Dutch company VOPAK Chemical Tankers, itself the result of a merger between Van Ommeren and Broere Shipping. 2008 saw the integration of the Broere and Essberger fleets as Essberger Tankers. In 2010 the company operated some 26 chemical tankers.

(Simon Smith)

Outside south-east Asia the Turkish port of Aliaga, located approximately 50km north of Izmir, is one of the most significant shipbreaking locations in the world. The refrigerated cargo ship **Medy** (then named **Myst**) was reported to have arrived at Aliaga for demolition in April 2006 under tow of the Danish tug **Suzanne A**. As illustrated by this photograph taken at Tuzla shipyard on 27 June 2006, demolition did not take place and the vessel was reprieved for further trading. **Mystic** was one of a pair of vessels produced by the Van Diepen shipyard at Waterhuizen for the Dutch reefer operator Seatrade. Relatively young for a reefer, the 1989-built vessel found her way to Aliaga as a result of a serious fire whilst she lay at the Gryfia ship repair yard at Szczecin in October 2005. Considered beyond economic repair and with her name shortened to **Myst**, she left Szczecin on 13 March 2006 bound for Aliaga via La Corunna. Reports indicate that she was beached at Aliaga but was pulled off some weeks later and towed to Tuzla for rebuilding. She left Tuzla in August 2007 following rebuilding as a general cargo ship, having adopted the Georgian flag and the name **Kaya**. A further renaming to **Kaya Pioneer** took place in 2008 with transfer to the Panamanian flag following some months later. Her operators are listed as Sea Pioneer Denizcilik ve Ticaret Ltd (registered owners Vandrana Management S.A.).

(Simon Smith)

Tuzla shipyard is active in both the repair and new build sectors. It is not unusual to see new and old vessels in close proximity as illustrated by the cement carrier *Naftocement III* and the tanker *Orasila* on 27 June 2006. Some thirty-six years separate the construction of the two vessels. *Naftocement III* is a product of Kanda Shipbuilding Co Ltd at Kure in Hiroshima prefecture. She was delivered to Japanese-flag owners as *Hokuyo Maru* in 1970. In 1997 she was sold and renamed *Little Cowboy* for Panama-flag owners. Acquisition by Piraeus-based Naftotrade Shipping & Commercial Co S.A. followed a year later when she took her current name. A transfer to the Maltese flag took place in 2007. Naftotrade operate some twenty bulk cement carriers primarily in the Mediterranean area. The chemical and oil products tanker *Orasila* was launched at Tuzla in 2006 by Desan Deniz. She has since been delivered to the Danish coastal tanker operator Rederiet M H Simonsen ApS. Seven of Simonsen's current fleet of nine vessels were products of Turkish shipyards. The *Orasila* passed through the Dardanelles on 7 September 2006 on her delivery voyage and has since spent a large part of her career trading in Greenland. In January 2009 she ran aground at Qaqortoq on the west coast of that country sustaining damage to her propeller. Repairs took place at Gdynia in February 2009 after which she returned to operation in Greenland.

(Simon Smith)

The Tuzla shipyard area contains a large number of vessels at any time with vessels in very close proximity to one another. Dockyard tugs are frequently in action moving vessels onto and from ship repair and construction berths. On 2 June 2008 the 16,750-tonne deadweight Turkish bulk carrier **Sibel Deval** is carefully manoeuvred onto a repair berth by the local tugs **Sanmar V** and **Sanmar VI**. The identical Robert Allan-designed tugs were built at Tuzla in 1995 and 1996. Sanmar was founded in Istanbul in 1976 and has since expanded to become a significant builder, delivering some eighty vessels to customers overseas and in Turkey. The first tug for Sanmar's own fleet, the

Sanmar I, was built at Tuzla in 1990. She left the Sanmar fleet in 2001 and is currently operating under the Kazakhstan flag. The current fleet contains eleven tugs providing towage services at various locations in the Black Sea, Mediterranean Sea and the Sea of Marmara, including the Bulgarian Black Sea port of Varna. The largest vessels delivered by Sanmar include the "Eskort" series, powerful twin Z-drive diesel-powered tugs. The first of these was delivered to Norwegian owner Östensjö Rederi A/S as **Vivax** in 2008. Two more of this class were delivered to Bugsier in 2009 as **Bugsier 9** and **Bugsier 10**.

(Simon Smith)

The St Vincent & the Grenadines-flagged general cargo ship **Syria Star** appears ready to return to service following dry-docking at Tuzla where she is seen on 12 August 2009. Indeed she sailed from Tuzla two days later and headed through the Bosphorus for the Russian Black Sea port of Novorossiysk to load a cargo for Alexandria. **Syria Star** is one of the numerous handysize general cargo ships delivered by Japanese yards in the 1970s, many of which remained in trade in 2010 despite the recent demolition frenzy. Her current name is her fifth. When delivered by Shin Kurushima Dockyard at Uwajima in 1977 she was named **Iris Island** for owners Josko KK. She continued to trade as such until 1986 when she became **Hollandic Confidence** for Andromeda Shipping Lines of Manila. After a period as **Hollandic** between 1990 and 1991 she reverted to

Hollandic Confidence until 1999. After various changes of registered ownership she was named **Mike M** for Greek owners listed as Odysea Carriers S.A. She took her current name and flag in 2006 following sale to Sea Rose Maritime LLC (registered owners Logan Shipholding Co). In March 1999 during her time as **Hollandic Confidence** she lost a hatch cover during a Pacific storm. She was assisted by the US Coastguard and arrived a day later at San Francisco where repairs took place. On 5 August 2010 **Syria Star** was reported hijacked in the Gulf of Aden but she was abandoned by the Somali pirates two days later and continued to trade at the end of 2010.

(Simon Smith)

The anchorage at Tuzla hosts a wide variety of shipping. 27 June 2006 was no exception and amongst the usual bulk carriers, tankers and general cargo ships was the research vessel **Fulmar**. Launched by Brooke Marine at Lowestoft as a Bulldog class hydrographic survey ship, she was the sixth Royal Navy vessel to bear the name **HMS Fawn** (pennant number A325). Three sisterships were commissioned during 1968, **HMS Beagle**, **HMS Bulldog** and **HMS Fox**. An improved version of the class, **HMS Roebuck**, was commissioned in 1986. **HMS Fox** was the first of the class to leave naval service, operating as **H.V. Fox** until 1998 when she was named **Plus Ultra** for Cayman Island flag interests. **HMS Bulldog** followed in 2001 when she was sold to Hong Kong-based interests for conversion to a yacht and she was renamed **Alyssa M II**. In April 2004 she suffered a serious fire at Nelson in New Zealand. She is reported to have sailed from Nelson in 2007 under tow of the tug **Svitzer Celeste** but was sold en route to a buyer in the Philippines who renamed her **Patricia Joyce**. **HMS Beagle** was disposed of in 2002, converted into a luxury yacht and named **Titan** under the Italian flag. She is currently operating in the Mediterranean. **HMS Fawn** left naval service in 1991 taking the name **Red Fulmar**. In 1998 she was sold to Seabulk International becoming **Seabulk Fulmar**. A sale to unknown owners in 2006 saw her name shortened to **Fulmar** and transfer to the North Korean flag. She is known to have arrived at Haifa in October 2007 for conversion to a yacht by Israeli Shipyards.

(Simon Smith)

Photographed at Tuzla Anchorage on 12 August 2009 is the general cargo ship *Güney Em*. She had previously passed through the Dardanelles from Iskenderun, a port situated on Turkey's Mediterranean coast, bound for Tuzla, on 22 June 2009. This vessel was built in 1979 as the *Saronic* for owners flying the flag of Greece, by the shipyard of Estaleiros EBIN/So S. A., based in Porto Alegre, Brazil. In 1985 her ownership passed to the UK, being renamed *Merchant Patriot* and owned by Cenargo Navigation Ltd. 1987 saw her sold to Armare Srl, of Naples, and flying the Italian flag as the *Chiaia di Luna*. She served these owners until 1991 when she passed to the Egyptian flag as *Ibn Khaldoun*, her owners being the Pan-Arab Shipping Co, of Alexandria. In 1996 she became *Blue Lagoon* flying the flag of Panama, followed by another name change to

her current name in 1999. Under the name of *Güney Em*, she has had a number of owners, but her commercial operators have remained unchanged. Unusually, she is operated by the Trans KA Tankers Management Co Ltd of Istanbul. As their name suggests, they manage a small fleet of tankers, all under the Turkish flag, as well as this single general cargo ship. Just prior to the photograph being taken, the *Güney Em* had transferred to the flag of Kiribati, being newly registered in Tarawa. She remained inactive in the anchorage until November 2009, when she was sold to Al Mortada Maritime Transport, based in the Lebanon. She was renamed *Almortada* under the Comoros flag and resumed trading in December 2009.

(Chris Brooks)

Until recently Chinese-built ships were not a particularly common sight in European and Mediterranean waters. The rapid expansion of shipbuilding in China has changed this as illustrated by the general cargo ship **Kanton** seen anchored off Tuzla on 2 June 2008. The **Kanton** is typical of a number of Chinese-built gearless general cargo vessels currently trading to Black Sea ports. She is a product of the Wenling Fangrong Shipyard located in China's Zhejiang province. Launched in 2006 as **Xing Long Zhou 73** she took her current name the same year following sale to Belize-based Poseidon Shipping. The same owners operate the sister vessel **Melwill** (launched at Wenling as **Xing Long Zhou 126**). Since transiting the Suez Canal in November 2007, the **Kanton** has traded exclusively in the Black Sea and Mediterranean. Illustrating the truly international nature of modern shipping, she flies the flag of the Polynesian Island of Tuvalu and is registered in Funafuti. With a population of just 12,000, Tuvalu is the third least populated world state. However, some 260 ships, with a gross tonnage of 1.4 million tons, are currently on the Tuvalu ship register (approximately one ship for every forty-six citizens!).

(Simon Smith)

The North Korean-flagged general cargo ship **Mu San** is seen at anchor off Tuzla on 2 June 2008. Launched in December 1980 by Neue Schlichting-Werft GmbH at Travemünde in West Germany she was delivered the following year to Djakarta Lloyd as **Sriwijaya**. Her sistership **Mataram** was delivered to Djakarta Lloyd later in 1981. After fifteen years service with the Indonesian state shipping line she was sold to Pacific International Lines (Private) Ltd and renamed **Kota Abadi** under the Singapore flag. **Mataram** was included in the same transaction and became **Kota Alam**. Both ships had a container capacity of 686 TEU. However, by 2003 Pacific International (PIL) had invested heavily in dedicated unitised tonnage and **Kota Abadi** was sold to North Korean interests as **Mu San**. Her owners are listed as Tonghae Sonbak Co Ltd. **Kota Alam** was disposed of by PIL in 2004 becoming **Oriental Carrier** for South Korean operators Sinokor Merchant Marine. In July 2009 she arrived at Jiangyin, China, for demolition. **Mu San** remains in service at the end of 2010.

(Simon Smith)

Anchored off Tuzla on 27 June 2006 the small Turkish ro-ro **Rize Ipekyolu** looks to have seen better days. In 1981 she was delivered to Norfolk Line as **Duke of Holland II** by the Dutch builder Amels Holland BV, of Makkum, and traded between Scheveningen and Great Yarmouth. Founded in 1961, Norfolk Line had entered the ferry business in 1969 with the acquisition of **Duke of Norfolk**, also a product of the Amels yard. **Duke of Norfolk** was disposed of in 1987 and continues to operate between Palm Beach and the Bahamas as the Honduran-flagged **Duke of Topsail**. In 1990 **Duke of Holland II** was renamed **Maersk Friesland**. In 1992 and 1993 she was chartered to Estline, operating between Tallinn and Stockholm. She left northern Europe in 1993 following sale to Adriatic RoRo Ltd, operating for Brodospas as **SV. Duje** under the St Vincent & the Grenadines flag. She operated across the Mediterranean until 2003 when she was sold to the Turkish company Rize Ipekyolu Deniz, and renamed **Rize Ipekyolu**. Between 2003 and 2005 she maintained a service between the Turkish Black Sea port of Rize and Poti in Georgia. Sale to other Turkish owners followed in 2008 when she became **Erdemler 8** for Marmara Sea ferry operators Erdemler Denizcilik.

(Simon Smith)

The container feeder ship **Zeeland** sits at anchor off Tuzla on 2 June 2008. She is one of five "AS-300" (300 TEU) type ships delivered to Ellerman Lines by Appledore Shipbuilders between 1978 and 1981. **City of Hartlepool** was the third vessel in the series, and traded as such under the UK flag until 1984, when she was chartered to Eimskip as **Laxfoss**. She returned to Ellerman a year later as **City of Manchester**. Ellerman was acquired by Andrew Weir in 1991. **City of Manchester** remained under Weir ownership until 2007 when she was sold to Turkish interests with her name shortened to **City** and registry transferred to the Netherlands Antilles. Renaming to **Zeeland** followed in the first half of 2008. A sale to Tartous-based Alfamarine Shipping Co Ltd in late 2009 saw her registered in Panama and renamed **Golden Bay**. Only one of **Zeeland**'s sisterships may remain, the Indonesia-flagged **Systemindo Perdana** (launched as **City of Oxford**), which was last reported in December 2008. Two of the other three vessels were total losses and one vessel went to Indian breakers in 2003.

(Simon Smith)

The St Kitts & Nevis-flagged coaster *Zenith* was at anchor off Tuzla on 2 June 2008. Movement reports suggest that she had been inactive for some time, although she did pass northbound through the Bosphorus a few days after the photograph was taken, on her way to the Russian port of Yeisk. She was built at the Westerbroek yard of E J Smit & Sons and was delivered to the Dutch short sea operator Brinkman Beheer BV as *Paul Brinkman* in 1983. A sale to Cypriot-flag owners in 1988 saw her renamed *Paola*. Dutch connections were restored in 1995 when she took the name *Michelle Trader* for

Arpa Shipping BV trading under the Maltese flag. After almost nine years with Arpa she was sold to Partner Co Ltd (registered owner Alabama Shipping Ltd) and became *Maxim* under the Dominican Republic flag. In late July 2004 she sailed from Hamburg and has since traded exclusively in the Mediterranean and Black Sea area. Her current name was registered just a few days before she was seen off Tuzla. Her current managers are listed as Solna Shipping & Trading Co (registered owner Maxim Shipping & Trading Inc).

(Simon Smith)

We now move onto the harbour at Pendik where a number of interesting vessels can usually be found, including laid up coasters and some unusual tugs. There is also a fast ferry service to Yalova from this harbour. Two tugs which seem to be regular occupants of the harbour are the **Pehlivan 2** and **Reis-6**. The **Pehlivan 2** dates back to 1980 when she was built at the Leninskaya Kuznitza Shipyard in Kiev, Ukraine. Completed as a fishing vessel, she was converted to a fishery research vessel in 1989. At some point since 1989 she has been converted to a tug / supply vessel. Until 2003 she was named **Tibiya** and owned by Kiyevskiy Inn Gidropriborov, of Kiev. She took the name of **Pehlivan 2** when she transferred from the Ukrainian to the Turkish flag with her new operators, Aras Salvage and Marine Constructions, residing in Tuzla. The **Reis-6** was completed at the Santierul Naval shipyard at Braila as the tug **Bran** in 1971. Her owners at this time were Navrom, the state shipping line of Romania. She continued under this ownership until 1993, when she transferred to Compania de Navigatie Maritime PETROMIN S.A. of Constantza, remaining under the Romanian flag. In 1999 she was sold to Mistral Maritime Services, and flying the Belize flag, was renamed **Mistral III**. She became **Reis** when she was sold to Aras Salvage and Marine Constructions in 2004, taking the Cambodian flag. Her final name change came in May 2007, when she became the **Reis-6**, flying the Turkish flag.

(Chris Brooks)

We now move on to the anchorage at Istanbul, situated just to the west of the southern entrance to the Bosphorus. This anchorage is used by vessels awaiting a northbound transit of the Bosphorus, as well as those awaiting orders and taking on bunkers and provisions. The small general cargo vessel *Al Hamed* is seen in Istanbul anchorage on 29 June 2006. In the 1950s and 1960s Hungarian shipyards produced large numbers of short sea vessels for the Soviet Union. *Al Hamed* was launched as *Otepya*, a product of the Angyalfold Works (also referred to as Ganz Danubius Shipyard & Crane Works) at Budapest and was one of a series of forty-five vessels known as the "Elva" type. *Otepya* continued to trade for the Estonian Shipping Co until her sale in 1993. As with many former Soviet Union vessels, she changed name and flag upon the dissolution of the USSR, becoming *Otepae* in 1992 and *Otepaa* a year later under the Estonian flag. From 1993 until 1998 she traded under the Honduran flag initially as *Smaragd* and later as *Hasan M* from 1996. A sale to Turkish owners in 1998 saw a further name change to *Reis*. Finally, in 2004 she became *Al Hamed*, at which point she flew the flag of North Korea. Two of the class have been the subject of controversy. Firstly, the *Baltic Sky* (originally *Artsiz*) was escorted to the small Greek port of Platiyali, having been raided by Greek special forces in June 2003, following the discovery that she was carrying undeclared explosives. Her current whereabouts are unknown. The *Al Hamed* became the subject of media reports herself in September 2007 with speculation that she was linked to Israeli air raids in Syria. The raids followed the alleged importation of an illicit cargo from North Korea on a ship that had berthed at Tartous. On 2 May 2008 the story came to an end when *Al Hamed* arrived at Aliaga for demolition.

(Simon Smith)

The refrigerated cargo vessel **African Warrior II** is seen in Istanbul anchorage on 29 June 2006. She is a product of the Miho Zosensho KK shipyard at Shimizu in Japan's Shizuoka prefecture. In 1978 she was delivered as **Souss** to the Moroccan company Société Marocaine de Navigation Frutière (SOFRUMA) for whom she traded under the Moroccan flag until 1994. A change of name to **Frio Monaco** followed a sale to Lomar Shipping Limited. 1996 saw a further change of name to **Frio Ionian** for operation by the Greek company Laskaridis under the Panamanian flag. In 2005 she was sold again, her registered owners being listed as Baffin Overseas SA. As **African Warrior II** she traded under the management of Aqua Azur Shipmanagement BV. In February 2009 she was transferred to the Moldovan flag and renamed **Taiba** following a sale to Jordanian interests. Since April 2010 she has flown the Tanzanian flag for Egyptian interests with official records indicating a conversion to a livestock carrier.

(Simon Smith)

A regular trader around the Baltic and northern European ports until early 2008, **Baltic Forest** is seen in the anchorage at Istanbul on 6 October 2008. She is instantly recognisable as a product of the Hugo Peters shipyard at Wewelsfleth, Germany, being launched in 1972 as **Ilse Wulff**, for owner, Hermann Wulff of Germany. **Ilse Wulff** retained her name until 1979 when she was sold to Minicarriers AB of Godby, Finland, renamed **Miniforest** and managed by Godby Shipping of Mariehamn. Under these owners she traded under the Finnish, Estonian and Belize flags. She passed to Maltese owners in 2000, but remained managed by Estonian and Finnish interests. In 2004 she was sold to Baltic Carrier Ltd of Dominica and renamed **Baltic Forest**, flying the Panamanian flag. **Baltic Forest** left her home waters in January 2008 for the Black Sea and the eastern Mediterranean. Following arrival in Turkish waters, she ran aground on 16 May 2008, near Çanakkale lighthouse, but was refloated a few hours later, with little damage. Shortly after the photograph was taken her flag was changed to that of St Kitts & Nevis. March 2009 saw her sold to Syrian-based owners, renamed **Gulf Forest** and flagged in Bolivia and later Tanzania. Under her new owners, she remains a regular visitor to the Bosphorus.

(Chris Brooks)

The Comoros-flagged general cargo ship **Best Line** was photographed in Istanbul anchorage on 1 June 2008. She is unusual in that having spent almost all of her career in Far Eastern waters from her delivery in 1984 until 2006, she has since migrated to the Mediterranean and Black Sea. She passed northbound through the Suez Canal in August 2006, her first port of call in the Mediterranean being Tartous. In late 2008 she was reported berthed at Haydarpasa following a cargo dispute involving the 3,000 tonnes of animal feed she was carrying. In November the situation deteriorated when a fire started in her No.1 hold. Further reports indicate that she was towed to the Pendik anchorage where she suffered a further fire in her No.2 hold some nine days later. By late January 2009 she had returned to Haydarpasa where she remained at the end of 2010 in poor condition, and with her cargo removed. **Best Line** was built at Guangzhou in 1984 and began her career as **Hong Qi 195** for Guangzhou Maritime Transport Group. In 1995 she became **Peng Fei** for owners listed as Tianjin Tianhe Shipping Co Ltd. She left the Chinese flag for Belize in 2003 when she took the name **Pan Ocean 9**. Her current name was adopted in 2004 after which followed transfer to the flags of North Korea and Comoros. **Best Line** is one of five sisterships completed by the Huangpu Shipyard at Guangzhou as **Hong Qi 193** to **Hong Qi 197** during 1984 and 1985. The other four vessels are all currently trading in the Far East, one having been converted to an asphalt tanker in 2005.

(Simon Smith)

The **Gefer Jabbarly** was completed in 1977 in the Navashinskiy Sudostroitelnyy Zavod "Oka" shipyard in Navashino. Upon completion she was named **Dzhafar Dzhabarly**, a name she carried until 1997, when she adopted her current name. She was one of a large class of "Kishinev" type vessels built at the Navashino shipyard, beginning with the name ship of the class in 1968. **Dzhafar Dzhabarly** was one of the last of 43 vessels of this class to be built. Her owners at the time of her completion were the Azerbaijan State Caspian Shipping Co based in Baku, Azerbaijan, but managed in Russia until 1992 and flying that country's flag . She remains owned by the Azerbaijan State Caspian Shipping Co but now flying the flag of Azerbaijan. Management was taken over by Meridian Shipping and Management of Baku in 2007. Vessels of this type are a relatively common sight in Istanbul and the Bosphorus – in fact, the Azerbaijan State Caspian Shipping Co still have ten of this class in their fleet. The last reported movement of the **Gefer Jabbarly** before being photographed in Istanbul anchorage on 10 August 2009 was her passage through the Dardanelles from Haifa on 13 June 2009, bound for the Black Sea for orders. She finally departed northbound for Mariupol later in the month. From Mariupol, she proceeded to Rostov-on-Don and then via the River Don, the Volgo-Don Canal and the River Volga, through to the Caspian Sea, bound for the Caspian coastline of Iran.

(Chris Brooks)

The Syrian-flagged **Luoay K** started life in Japan at the Hashihama Zosen shipyard at Imabari where she was completed in 1977. At this point she started a long period trading under the Greek flag as the **Manthos** for the Manthos Primera Shipping Co of Panama. She remained under this ownership until 1995 when she was renamed **Captain Giannis** under the Cypriot flag. In 2004 she was again sold, this time to Shield Commercial of Dominica, renamed **Kori** and transferred initially to the flag of Dominica. Shortly afterwards, her flag was changed to that of Panama. Her final name change came in February 2006 when she became the **Luoay K** under the flag of Syria. Her owners at this time became the Luoay Shipping and Trading Co Ltd with her port of registry being Lattakia. She was photographed on 25 June 2006 in the anchorage at Istanbul, whilst waiting to transit the Bosphorus northbound to Novorossiysk. She had arrived in the anchorage from Gabes, Tunisia, earlier that day. Since the photograph was taken, her trading pattern has predominantly been between ports in the Black Sea and ports in Syria, Algeria and Tunisia. Thus, she is a regular visitor to the Bosphorus area.

(Chris Brooks)

The **Poisk** is listed as a general cargo ship having been converted from a research vessel at some point in her career. She was built in 1974 at the Khabarovsk Shipyard at Khabarovsk, in the far east of Russia. Completed as a vessel of the "Valerian Uryvayev" type, she was one of the first of this large class of twenty research ships built between 1974 and 1984. All were built at Khabarovsk. The **Poisk** transferred to Ukrainian registry in 1988. Since that time, the **Poisk** is one of a number of former research vessels that have traded between Istanbul and ports in the Ukraine, including Odessa, Kherson, Yevpatoriya, Illichivsk and Belgorod-Dnestrovskiy. They can often be seen moored in the harbour at Zeytinburnu, Istanbul, or sometimes berthed at the cruise terminal. She is seen in Istanbul anchorage on 1 June 2008, at which point she was operating a regular service between Belgorod-Dnestrovskiy and Istanbul, arriving at Belgorod-Dnestrovskiy on 7 June. One has to question the viability of this type of vessel as a general cargo vessel, as they were built with only one small hold, served by two 1.5-tonne derricks. Vessels employed on this service can often be seen on arrival at Istanbul with cargo piled high on their decks, utilising every available space.

(Chris Brooks)

Many coasters built in northern Europe are sold to owners trading in the Black Sea and Mediterranean as European owners upgrade their fleets with newer ships. A typical example is the Danish-built **Sea Arrow** seen at anchor off Istanbul on 1 June 2008. **Andreas Boye** was one of five sisterships delivered by A/S Nordsøværftet at Ringkøbing to Danish owners between 1979 and 1981. She continued to trade worldwide for Hermann C Boye & Co until 2002 when she was laid up at Marstal for thirteen months. A sale to Egypt Trade Maritime Services (registered owner Indian Summer Nav Ltd) followed in 2003 and she took the name **Al Furkan** under the Georgian flag. Several further changes of management and ownership have since been recorded with name changes to **Andreas** in 2006 and **Sea Arrow** in 2008. Since being photographed in 2008,

she has transferred from the Sierra Leone to the Comoros Islands flag. **Sea Arrow**'s four sisterships have spread out far and wide. The first vessel, delivered as **Alice Trigon**, was sold to Vietnamese owners in 1996 and was last reported in 2005 as **Hai Dang-04**. The **Inger M** changed names a number of times and was last reported after release from detention in Tunisia in 2008 as the Libyan flag **Assafa**. The **Elisabeth Vesta** was eventually sold to Indian owners in 2004 and as **Maanav Star** became the subject of a rescue operation when she ran hard aground on a Sussex beach on her delivery voyage. Fleetmate **Hermann C Boye** became **Lady Lotmore II** in 2002 and is currently operating out of Miami.

(Simon Smith)

The Austin & Pickersgill-built SD-14 type general cargo ship **Tania** was anchored light off Istanbul on 25 June 2006. More than 200 of the standard design and licence-built derivatives were produced by British and other builders in Argentina, Brazil and Greece. Twenty years elapsed between the delivery of the first vessel, **Nicola**, and completion of the last at Rio de Janeiro in 1988. The **Tania** is one of 126 of the design built at Sunderland. She was launched as **Empros** on 10 November 1977 and delivered to Empros Lines (George Dracopoulos) the following year. An inauspicious start to her career saw a collision on the River Schelde with the general cargo ship **Mariann Gem**, which subsequently sank. Thereafter she maintained the regular Empros Lines service between eastern Mediterranean ports and the continent. With a decline in demand for break bulk services, her last sailing from Antwerp was on 18 June 2003. A sale to WVP Shipping SA (managers Admiral Ship Management) soon followed and she took the name **Tania** under the Georgian flag. When photographed she was in the process of her second renaming, the new name **QSM Dubai** being visible on the bridge board. On 2 June 2010 the **QSM Dubai** was hijacked in the Gulf of Aden. The following day the ship was stormed by Somali land troops and sadly the captain died during the operation.

(Simon Smith)

The general cargo ship **TK Odessa** belongs to the large fleet of Kiran Holdings, a Turkish company operating a number of general cargo ships and bulk carriers. In addition, the company also operates one of the largest shipyards in Tuzla. Members of this fleet of ships are regular visitors to the Bosphorus. The **TK Odessa** began life in 1982 at the Daedong Shipbuilding Co Ltd at Busan, South Korea. Launched as the **Ocean Splendor**, she carried this name until 1989 when she was renamed **Ocean Rider**. At this time she was owned by Ocean Rider Maritime SA, of Panama, flying the Panamanian flag. She was, however, managed by the Hokusho Shipping Co Ltd of Kobe, Japan. In 1994 she reverted to her original name, **Ocean Splendor**, coming under the control of the Setouchi Marine Co Ltd of Hiroshima, Japan. In May 1995, she was again sold, this time out of Japanese management to Malaysian owners and renamed **Melinau Empat**. She remained with her Malaysian owners, Shinline Sendirian Berhad, until 1998 when she transferred to the flag of Malta. At this time she came under the control of Kıran Makina ve Gemi Sanayii Turgut Kıran, part of the Kiran Holdings group. Her current owners are listed as Princess Overseas Shipping Ltd, of Malta. She was photographed in the anchorage at Istanbul on 10 August 2009, waiting to transit the Bosphorus whilst on a voyage from Ashdod in Israel to Galatz in Romania.

(Chris Brooks)

Turning our attention to vessels making their Bosphorus transit we now arrive at the southernmost part of the Bosphorus. This is the busiest section of the Bosphorus with the city of Istanbul straddling the waterway. As well as cargo ships making their transit, a plethora of ferries criss-cross the stretch of water between the Asian and European sides of the city. The **A. Bryukhovetskiy** is seen approaching Istanbul from the Sea of Marmara before making her northbound transit of the Bosphorus on 8 July 2007. At the time, she was on a voyage from Bandırma to Azov, a Russian port situated sixteen kilometres from the mouth of the River Don, which flows into the Sea of Azov. The **A. Bryukhovetskiy** was built at the Navashinskiy Sudostroitelnyy Zavod "Oka" yard at Navashino, a town on the banks of the Oka River, one of the tributaries of the River

Volga. She was completed in January 1979 as **Volgo-Don 227**, one of the very large class of sea-river vessels. At some point she was renamed **A. Belodvortsev**, before becoming **A. Bryukhovetskiy** in July 2003. For ten years, from 1993 to 2003 she flew the flag of Ukraine, but reverted to the Russian flag upon her renaming in 2003. The vessel is currently owned by the Don River Shipping Joint-Stock Co (Donrechflot) of Rostov-on-Don, but managed by the Volga-Don Joint Stock Shipping Co also based in Rostov-on-Don. This ship is a regular sight at Istanbul, as she trades mainly around ports in the Black Sea and Turkey, with occasional voyages to other countries in the eastern Mediterranean.

(Chris Brooks)

The elderly containership **Destiny** approaches the end of her southbound Bosphorus transit on 25 June 2006. She has maintained a regular service between Turkish ports and Constantza from 2004 until the present time. In 1970 the British Railways Board took delivery of a pair of 182 TEU capacity containerships from the Verolme Cork Dockyard. **Brian Boroime** and **Rhodri Mawr** were delivered for operation on Irish Sea services from the new Holyhead Freightliner Terminal and Heysham to Dublin and Belfast. The growth in roll-on/roll-off freight resulted in the cessation of the dedicated container service in 1989. By then the sisterships had seen ownership with Sealink, formed by British Railways in 1979, and Sea Containers to whom Sealink was sold in 1984. The pair were acquired by the Greek company Sarlis Container Services SA in 1990 operating under the Cypriot flag as **Peltainer** and **Peliner**, names they retained until 2004. The **Peltainer** was sold to North Korean flag interests as **Abdul H** and she continues to trade in the Black Sea. She was transferred to Sierra Leone registry in 2007. The **Peliner** took the name **Ral Destiny**, also under the North Korean flag, operating for Karachi-based Tomini Ship Management. Her name was shortened to **Destiny** a few months later when she took the Comoros Islands flag. The **Destiny** was renamed **Yamm** in September 2009.

(Simon Smith)

Here we see an example of the "Kaliningrad" class of sea-river ships, built at the Zavody Tazkeho Strojarstva (ZTS), shipyard in Komarno, in what was then Czechoslovakia. The **Endo Moon** was completed in 1968, originally named **Tuapse**. She kept this name until 1994 when she was shortened by 18 metres, to have an overall length of 85,06 metres, and converted for seagoing operations. At this point she received the name of **Julius**, under the flags of Estonia and later Lithuania with the ownership listed as the Vortika Shipping Co Ltd of Klaipeda. In 1999 she was renamed **Sea Walker**, under the Belize flag, followed by **Marwa M** in 2001, flying the flag of Tonga but owned by Egyptian interests. It was under this name that her anchor damaged a submarine cable off Malta on 25 November 2001. She was escorted into Valletta, arrested and laid up in port. Subsequently sold in auction in 2003 to Cassar Ship Repair of Valletta, she remained in Valletta until July 2005, by which time her owners were the Redmond Shipping Co Ltd. In 2006 she was sold to Endo Star Inc and renamed **Endo Moon**, her new managers being the Aktug Shipping and Trading Co, of Istanbul. It is as the **Endo Moon** that we see this vessel approaching the Bosphorus at Istanbul, on 8 July 2007, whilst on a northbound voyage from Diliskelesi in Turkey to Novorossiysk.

(Chris Brooks)

With afternoon sunshine on her distinctive lime green hull, Bergesen's LPG tanker **Havdrott** exits the Bosphorus on 24 June 2006. On passage from Yuzhnyy to the US Gulf, she would have less than a year to trade before her final arrival on a Chittagong beach in June 2007. The second of a four ship order from P&O's Bulk Shipping Division she was delivered in 1976 by the Emden Thyssen Nordseewerke yard as **Galpara**. The remainder of the quartet were delivered as **Garinda**, **Galconda** and **Garala**. A sale to the Norwegian company Havtor A/S saw **Garinda** and **Garala** assume the names **Hekabe** and **Hemina** in 1986. The following year **Galpara** and **Galconda** took the Havtor names **Havdrott** and **Havkong**. All four ships left the UK register for the Bermuda flag in 1991, a further transfer to the Bahamas flag following six years later. In the meantime Havtor and Bergesen had merged. **Hekabe** joined the Norwegian International Register in the year 2000, the other three vessels followed in 2001. By October 2009 all four ships had been delivered to Asian breakers. **Havdrott** was the first, arriving at Chittagong Roads on 5 June 2007 and she was beached two days later. **Hemina**, the only one of the quartet to have adopted the corporate nomenclature as **BW Hemina** in 2007, went to Alang in July 2009. Both **Havkong** and **Hekabe** arrived at Chittagong in October 2009.

(Simon Smith)

The geared bulk carrier **Ocean Beauty** passes Istanbul on her way from the Black Sea to Croatia on 27 June 2006. She is one of numerous bulk carriers delivered in the 1970s by shipyards in the north-east of the UK for British owners. The Swan Hunter yard at Hebburn on the River Tyne delivered the **Trinculo** to Bowring Steamship Co Ltd in 1978. A sistership, **Desdemona**, was delivered to Bowring in the same year. In 1984 she took the name **Bijela** for Monaco-based interests under the St Vincent & the Grenadines flag. She became **Boka** in 1987 and **Sumadija** a year later when she adopted the Yugoslav flag for Jugoslavenska Oceanska Plovidba, listed as her commercial operator until 2003. 1996 saw two further name changes and a return to the St Vincent & the Grenadines flag, firstly to **Marie B** and later in the year to **Novi**. In 2003 she became **Argola** for Croatian interests. Syrian owners, Al Fahel Shipping, purchased her in 2005 and named her **Ocean Beauty**. In 2008 she was renamed **FGM Achiever**, although the funnel colours on the photograph would suggest an earlier association with FGM Ship Management. In late 2009 she was reported sold to Bangladeshi shipbreakers but early in 2010 she became **Utlo Ma Uhia** for interests in Singapore. This proved to be a temporary reprieve and she was beached at Chittagong in November 2010. Sistership **Desdemona** also took the name **Boka** and subsequently **Suibicevac**, **Achilles**, **Diana Z** and **Bright Future** before her sale to her current North Korean owners as **Mi Rae** in 2003.

(Simon Smith)

The general cargo vessel **Sancris** was seen approaching the southern entrance to the Bosphorus early in the morning of 8 July 2007. At the time of the photograph, she was on a voyage from Güllük, on the Mediterranean coast of Turkey to Odessa. The **Sancris** dates back to 1975, when she was built as the **Busteni** at the Santierul Naval Galati shipyard at Galatz, Romania. She was one of approximately sixty vessels of this type built at Galatz, Tulcea and Braila over an extended period of time. Originally belonging to the fleet of Navrom, the Romanian state-owned shipping company, she remained with this company until 1990 when she was taken over by CNM Romline Shipping Co SA of Constantza. In 1997 she was purchased by Interocean Services Srl of Bucharest, and renamed **Ocean Line 1** continuing to fly the Romanian flag. Her final name change came in the year 2000 when she was purchased by Naval Heritage Maritime and renamed **Sancris**. At this point she was transferred to the flag of Bolivia, before changing to the Panamanian flag in 2001. Shortly after this photograph was taken she made one last trip through the Bosphorus on 25 July 2007, bound for Jeddah via the Suez Canal. From Jeddah she proceeded to Jebel Ali, UAE and then Sohar, Oman, before arriving on 24 September 2007 at Gadani Beach, Pakistan for breaking.

(Chris Brooks)

Most Istanbul residents would have been oblivious to the elegant shape of **Santos Star** as she neared completion of her final Bosphorus passage on 25 June 2006. She was to call at Eleusis before transiting the Suez Canal on her way to Chittagong, where, two months after this photograph was taken, she was driven onto the beach for demolition. She was one of a class of eight large Snow class reefers built at La Ciotat between 1972 and 1974 for Swedish operator Sven Salen. All eight were delivered with "Snow" names, the second vessel, **Snow Flake**, was delivered in 1972. In 1984 she was sold to Hong Kong-based South View Shipping Ltd (managers Whitwill, Cole & Co Ltd) and was named **South View** under the Panamanian flag. A year later she transferred to the Hong Kong flag under the name **Blue Sea**, a name she had for just a couple of weeks before becoming **Santos Star** for the first time. By the end of 1986 she was trading as **Limari** but reverted back to **Santos Star** in the summer of 1987, sailing under the Singapore flag. Following transfer to the Bahamas flag in 1994, her penultimate name change took place in 1996, when she became **Snow Delta**, before reverting once again to **Santos Star** in 2000. From late 1998 until sale to Bangladeshi breakers in 2006 her owners were quoted as Athens-based Target Marine SA (registered owner Lyford Shipping Inc). In 2002 she was laid-up for some three and a half months in the River Fal. By the end of 2010 **Snow Drift** was the sole survivor of the class. Two vessels were sold to Iran in 1985 and went to Indian breakers in 1998 and 2000. **Snow Flower** was demolished at Alang in 2008 and **Santiago Star** (delivered as **Snow Ball**) was beached at Chittagong on 28 August 2006, one day after **Santos Star**. Both **Snow Crystal** and **Snow Land** went to Indian breakers in 2010.

(Simon Smith)

Throughout the 1970s, Scandinavian shipyards produced significant numbers of refrigerated cargo ships. A typical example is the *Tropical Land*, seen as she is about to exit the Bosphorus on 27 June 2006. Nylands Verksted delivered her as *Maranga* to London-based Sogar Shipping Co Ltd in 1972. She was one of five sisterships built between 1971 and 1975, the first by Bergens at Bergen and the remaining four vessels by Nylands at Oslo. The ships were part of a class known as "Super Core" ordered by the Israeli company Maritime Fruit Carriers. Within a year she was sold and renamed *Brunsland* under the West German flag for the Frigomaris Shipping GmbH of Hamburg. In 1978 she took the name *Tropical Land* for the first time under the Liberian flag. Transfer to the Ecuadorian flag followed in 1984, although she was managed by Oslo-based Irgens Larsen A/S. In 1986 she was renamed *Rio Guayas*, remaining under the Ecuadorian flag until 1997, when she reverted to *Tropical Land*, upon sale to Tropical Navigation (Malta) Ltd. From 1991 until her sale to Bangladeshi breakers in 2008, she was managed by Dole Fresh Fruit International Ltd whose ship management arm is known as Reefership Marine Services Ltd. In May 2008 she passed through the Suez Canal, arriving at Chittagong Roads on 13 June, having been renamed *Tropical Sand* and registered under the Sierra Leone flag. Beaching followed six days later. By the end of the year 2000 Indian breakers had already demolished three of the sisterships. The first vessel of the class, named *Morillo* throughout her lifetime, arrived at Alang in July 2008. The class was consigned to history when the final ship, *Cherry*, was beached at Mumbai on 19 September 2009.

(Simon Smith)

The cruise ship **Aegean Two** leaves the cruise terminal at Istanbul in fading light on 6 October 2007. She was launched in August 1956 by Cantieri Riuniti dell'Adriatico at Monfalcone and delivered to Adriatica Lines as **Ausonia** the following September for service between Trieste and Beirut. In the late 1970s **Ausonia** was refitted at San Marco by Arsenale Triestino SpA and her passenger capacity increased for cruising. In 1983 she was acquired by Ausonia Crociere SpA, a subsidiary of Grimaldi. During 1986 her passenger capacity was further increased and some alterations made to her superstructure. The Cypriot operator Louis Cruise Lines purchased the vessel in 1998. She retained her name until 2006 when she became the **Ivory**, also changing from the Cypriot to the Greek flag. A further change to **Aegean Two** followed a year later. By early 2008 she had reverted to the name **Ivory** and after a season of cruises in the eastern Mediterranean she arrived at Eleusis in October 2008 for lay up. An inevitable sale to Indian breakers followed. Her final voyage as **Winner 5** under the St Kitts & Nevis flag saw her arrive off Alang on 2 March 2010, beaching taking place two days later.

(Simon Smith)

The Tea Gardens at Gülhane Park, Istanbul, provide a good vantage point from which to watch shipping transiting the Bosphorus as well as the cruise ship movements at the Yolcu Salonu cruise terminal, Karaköy. Here we see the veteran cruise ship **Blue Monarch**, departing for Rhodes in the late afternoon sunshine on 8 July 2007. She had arrived earlier that day from Piraeus. The **Blue Monarch** was built as the **Renaissance** in 1966 at Chantiers de l'Atlantique, St. Nazaire, for Compagnie Française de Navigation. She subsequently carried the names **Homeric Renaissance**, **World Renaissance**, **Awani Dream**, **World Renaissance**, and **Grand Victoria**, in that order, for several owners. In 2007 she was sold to Blue Monarch Shipping Inc, of Madeira, and has since that time, operated under the Monarch Classic Cruises banner, as **Blue Monarch**. For Monarch Classic Cruises she mainly operated weekly cruises out of Piraeus calling at various Greek and Turkish ports. By the end of 2008 she was laid up at Perama. Sold to Indian shipbreakers in January 2010, she sailed from Piraeus as the Sierra Leone-flagged **Maestro** in March of that year. Suffering mechanical failure on her delivery voyage, it was not until 11 August 2010 that she was finally driven ashore at Alang.

(Chris Brooks)

Seen berthed at the Yolcu Salonu cruise terminal in Istanbul on 9 October 2008, is the veteran cruise ship **Ocean Monarch**. She had arrived earlier in the day from Varna. Later the same day she departed bound for Santorini. **Ocean Monarch** was built in 1955 by Swan Hunter and Wigham Richardson at Wallsend on Tyne, as the passenger-cargo vessel **Port Sydney**. She was initially employed on Port Line's United Kingdom to Australia services. Together with her sistership **Port Melbourne**, she was sold in 1972 to Greek interests for conversion into passenger ferries. She was actually rebuilt as the cruise ship **Daphne**, for Delian Cruises and entered service in 1975. Shortly afterwards, she was chartered to Costa Line, and eventually purchased by them. Costa operated her under the Prestige Cruises management, alongside her sistership, by now renamed

Danae, until 1996. **Daphne** was renamed **Switzerland** in 1996 when she was sold to Swiss-based Leisure Cruises. In 2002 she was briefly renamed **Ocean Odyssey**, and then **Ocean Monarch** when she was sold to Majestic International Cruises. During the period from 2002 to 2008, she has operated for Page and Moy, Hansa Kreuzfahrten and Golden Star Cruises. Majestic International Cruises sold her in 2008 to World Cruises Agency based in Portugal. Shortly after the photograph was taken, she was renamed **Princess Daphne**, joining her sistership, now renamed **Princess Danae** under the banner of Classic International Cruises. The fact that both sisters are still going strong after over fifty years of service bears testament to the quality of construction of these vessels on the Tyne all those years ago.

(Chris Brooks)

The cruise terminal at Istanbul is visited by a wide variety of vessels. The contrasting styles of *Omega G* and *The Calypso* were evident on 5 October 2007. *Omega G* was delivered to the USSR in 1965 as the "Nikolay Zubov" class (Project 850M) research ship *Faddey Belingsgausen*. Szczecin Shipyard delivered eight of the oceanographic research ships between 1964 and 1968. Renamed *Omega* by 1996, she has operated a regular service between the Ukranian port of Yalta and Istanbul since 2001. A name change to *Omega G* in 2005 coincided with transfer to the Comoros Islands flag and a sale to Anguilla-based Granada Logistics SA. At some time prior to 2001 she was converted into a passenger/general cargo ship, although official sources record her as a passenger (cruise) ship. The cruise ship *The Calypso* is a product of Italcantieri at Castellammare di Stabia. She entered service in 1967 as the car ferry *Canguro Verde*, trading in the western Mediterranean until her sale to Saudi Arabian owners in 1981. She

operated under the Saudi flag as *Durr* until 1989 when she returned to Mediterranean waters as *Ionian Harmony* for Strintzis Lines. A further sale to Bahamas interests in 1990 resulted in a move to the Caribbean and the name *Sun Fiesta*. In 1992 she returned to Piraeus for conversion to a cruise ship and was acquired by Regency Cruises as *Regent Jewel*. She was subsequently chartered to Jule Cruises of Nassau as *Calypso* in 1994. Louis Cruise Lines acquired her in 2000, the change of name to *The Calypso* followed in 2005. In 2006 she suffered an engine room fire whilst off Beachy Head. The fire was quickly extinguished and she was safely towed to Southampton for repairs. After two years operating cruises for Thomson under Louis Lines management she completed her final cruise for Thomson in October 2009. She operated cruises from Limassol for Louis Lines during 2010.

(Simon Smith)

The **Sevastopol-1**, seen at the cruise terminal at Istanbul on 9 October 2008, runs a regular passenger and cargo service from Sevastopol in the Ukraine to Istanbul. She has been employed on this service since 2001, and is one of a number of former Soviet research ships, which maintain this trade between Istanbul and the Ukraine. General cargo can be seen stowed on her stern under tarpaulins and nets. **Sevastopol-1** was completed at the Stocznia Szczecinska shipyard at Szczecin in 1968 as the research vessel **Musson**. She was one of the first of a class of nine "Passat" type vessels, built from 1968 to 1971. She was renamed **Sevastopol-1** in 1999 when she was converted from a research vessel to a passenger ship. During this conversion accommodation was provided for 100 passengers. At this time she is listed as being under the ownership of the Ukrainian Scientific Centre of the Ecology of Sea, based in Odessa. In 2000 she was briefly owned by Gess and Co in Sevastopol. Her ownership was transferred in 2001 to the Ukraine Marine Ecology Research Centre in Odessa, who are listed as her current owners. How this ownership ties in with a passenger and cargo service to Istanbul remains to be seen.

(Chris Brooks)

With all the attractions that Istanbul has to offer it is no surprise that many cruise operators incorporate the city into their itineraries. Present on 1 June 2008 was the Pullmantur Cruise ship *Sky Wonder*. She is notable as being the last sizeable steam turbine powered passenger ship constructed. A product of the Chantiers du Nord et de la Mediterranée yard at La Seyne-sur-Mer near Toulon she was delivered to Sitmar in 1984 as *Fairsky*, sailing under the Liberian flag. Following the purchase of Sitmar by Princess Cruises in 1988 she flew the Red Ensign and took the name *Sky Princess*. In the autumn of 2000 she was transferred to P&O Cruises Australia and renamed *Pacific Sky*. Pullmantur acquired her for the 2006 season renaming her *Sky Wonder* in May of that year. She operated in the eastern Mediterranean for three seasons with Pullmantur but migrated to South America during the northern hemisphere winters. Although continuing to operate for Pullmantur, 2009 saw a change of scene to the western Mediterranean and with it the new name of *Atlantic Star*. Her employment proved to be short-lived and lengthy periods of inactivity have followed. At the end of 2010 she remained laid-up at Marseilles. In recent years several cruises have had to be cancelled due to mechanical failure and other incidents. The most serious of these was a grounding off the Turkish port of Kusadası in March 2008. Local tugs took four days to refloat the vessel.

(Simon Smith)

34

Most vessels photographed underway at Istanbul are in transit to or from Black Sea ports. However, Istanbul's port of Haydarpasa, sometimes referred to as Haidar Pasha, is a busy port in its own right. The terminals at Haydarpasa are operated by Turkish State Railways and handle a wide range of vessels including general cargo, roll-on/roll-off and container ships. The container terminal is capable of handling up to 1200 vessels a year and some 144,000 TEU of containerised cargo. Frequent callers at Haydarpasa are the distinctively coloured containerships of Turkon Container Transportation and Shipping.

As indicated by the funnel colours, the line was established by the Kasif Kalkavan Group in 1997. Turkon operate a modern fleet of Turkish-built containerships and call at ports in the Mediterranean, Israel, Europe and North America. Turkon's *Alkın Kalkavan* is seen making her approach to Haydarpasa on 2 June 2008 having arrived from the nearby port of Ambarli. The letters "MCL" on the vessel's hull indicate that she is operated by MCL Feeders Ltd. A product of Tuzla's Sedef yard she was delivered in late 2006 and has since operated exclusively in the Mediterranean.

(Simon Smith)

In her thirty-first year Maersk Line's Panamax containership ***Ankara*** was in the later stages of her career when photographed at Istanbul's Haydarpasa terminal on 27 June 2006. She was one of a series of six 1200 TEU "A-class" vessels built at Hamburg by Blohm and Voss for Maersk. A further three of the class were built by Flenderwerft at Lübeck. All of the vessels were lengthened in 1978. During the 1980s a major conversion programme took place in Japan during which a number of bow and stern sections were exchanged with the reconstructed vessels generally assuming the name of the bow section. Three ships were equipped with quarter stern doors and ramps. The original steam turbines were replaced with diesel engines. ***Anders Maersk*** emerged from conversion in 1984 as ***Anna Maersk*** with her container capacity increased to 1984 TEU. In 1998 ***Anna Maersk*** was renamed ***Maersk Bahrain***, a name she retained until becoming ***Ankara*** in 2004. In February 2009 she was delivered to Pakistani breakers at Gadani Beach. During 1994 two of the Blohm and Voss-built vessels were chartered to the United States Navy's Sealift Command, undergoing conversion at Sparrows Point shipyard in Maryland. Following service with the US military, both vessels were sold to the Italian line Ignazio Messina as ***Jolly Arancione*** and ***Jolly Nero*** in 2006 and are now the only survivors from the class of nine. Four of the Blohm and Voss-built vessels continued in service with Maersk Line until late in 2008 when two of the class were delivered to Asian breakers. The last of the quartet was renamed ***Maersk Belawan*** in 1998 and ***Bella 1*** in 2008 before going to Chinese breakers a year later.

(Simon Smith)

The world of shipping can change fast, as illustrated by the **YM Longevity**, one of eleven 2054 TEU sisterships built for Yang Ming Line between 1980 and 1983 by China Shipbuilding Corporation at Kaoshiung. All trading at the start of 2008, ten of the class had been delivered to breakers by the end of January 2009. The sole survivor, delivered as **Ming Universe**, was converted to a livestock carrier in 2002 and continues to trade as **Ocean Shearer**. The first seven vessels provided a Far East to USA service from 1980. With the delivery of the remaining four vessels services were expanded to cover the Mediterranean and northern Europe. Whilst Yang Ming remained owners throughout the vessels' careers they operated under various names whilst on charter. **Ming Longevity** had spells as **Maersk Jeddah**, **Med Hong Kong** and **Gibraltar Bridge** before reverting to **Ming Longevity** in 1998. The majority of the class adopted corporate nomenclature in 2004 as did **YM Longevity**. From 2003 the vessel maintained a service between the Mediterranean, Turkey and the Far East. She passed through the Dardanelles for the last time on 30 November 2008 and arrived at Xinhui on 29 December for breaking. She is seen at Haydarpasa on 2 June 2008.

(Simon Smith)

A typically busy Bosphorus provides the backdrop to the bulk carrier **Boron** as she makes a northbound passage on 26 June 2006. At thirty-seven years of age the Danish-built vessel was approaching the end of her career. She was sailing in ballast from Ortona for Mariupol. By 1 September she had anchored off Alang. Beaching took place five days later. Launched in 1969 at Naskskov Skibsværft, she was delivered to the Polish Steamship Company (Polska Zegluga Morska) as **Kopalnia Kleofas**. In 1995 she transferred to the Marshall Islands flag and shortened her name to **Kleofas** but continued to operate for Polsteam. After sale to the Syrian operator Riamar in 1999, she took the name **Boron**. When photographed **Boron** was one of two surviving sisters from seven vessels delivered to PZM by Nakskov in 1968 and 1969. **Sorbo**, originally **Kopalnia Szczyglowice**, arrived at Alang in August 2006. The other five sisterships were delivered to Asian breakers between 1997 and 2001.

(Simon Smith)

The elegant lines of the yacht **Savarona** grace the Bosphorus on 5 October 2007. She was built by Blohm and Voss at Hamburg in 1931 for the granddaughter of the Brooklyn Bridge engineer John Roebling, Mrs Emily Roebling-Cadwallader. Unable to visit the United States due to potentially crippling import duties, the ship was sold to the Turkish Government in 1938 for one million dollars, a quarter of her construction cost. Her purchase was believed to have resulted from an incident in 1936 aboard the Turkish yacht **Ertugrul**, when the visiting King Edward VII had his flannels dirtied by soot from the yacht's smokestack. Atatürk ordered the demolition of the **Ertugrul** and the purchase of a suitable replacement. **Savarona** arrived in Istanbul in May 1938 and hosted cabinet meetings until Atatürk's death in November 1938. She remained inactive, lying in Kanlıca Bay until 1951 when the Turkish Navy utilised her as a training ship. She was reported to have been named **Günes Dil** during this period. In 1979 she was gutted by fire at the Turkish Naval Academy in the Sea of Marmara and lay virtually abandoned for ten years. Saved from demolition by the Turkish businessman Kahraman Sadıkoglu, a three-year, twenty-five million dollar refurbishment programme followed at Tuzla Shipyard. A lavish interior was designed by Donald Starkey. She is equipped with a large swimming pool, two jacuzzis, two saunas and steam rooms, a fitness centre and a floor-heated Turkish bath built from 260 tons of carved marble. Pride of place goes to an eighty-six metre gold-trimmed staircase that survived from her original construction. Her original steam turbine engines were replaced by twin eight-cylinder 3,600bhp Caterpillar diesel engines.

(Simon Smith)

The early morning mist has almost cleared as the combined bulk/oil carrier **Alkman** heads northbound through the Bosphorus. She is seen approaching the Bosphorus Bridge in ballast on 28 June 2006. She was on passage from Greece to load at the Bulgarian port of Bourgas. **Cougar** and **Jaguar** were delivered by Namura Shipbuilding Co Ltd of Imari in 1985 and have since followed similar career paths. 1988 saw a transfer to the UK flag as **Sioux** and **Siksita** for Gibraltar-based interests. One year later the pair were sold to Uddevalla Shipping and renamed **Nor-Obo 7** and **Nor-Obo 8** under the Norwegian flag. Before the end of 1989 further changes of identity resulted in the names **Obo Harrier** and **Obo Hawk**. By the autumn of 1990 the standard nomenclature of Frontline had been adopted as **Front Harrier** and **Front Hawk**. In 1996 the sisters were sold to the London-based Greek owners Lyras Maritime Ltd taking the names **Alkaios** and **Alkman**, transferring to the Bahamas flag by the spring of 1997. At the end of 2010 **Alkman** continued to operate for Lyras. In late 2009 **Alkaios** was sold to Chinese interests and was renamed **Lucky Rainbow** under the Panamanian flag.

(Simon Smith)

To the north of the Bosphorus Bridge is the small suburb of Kandilli. Several vantage points exist here, from which it is possible to photograph the northbound convoy of vessels travelling through the Bosphorus during the morning. The large crude oil tankers transiting the Bosphorus are an impressive sight, especially when they are empty and riding high in the water. An example is the *Aegean Horizon* which had passed beneath the Bosphorus Bridge and is seen proceeding northwards past Kandilli. She was photographed whilst on a voyage from Trieste to Novorossiysk on 10 October 2008. This was one of many voyages she has undertaken, exporting oil from Novorossiysk to ports mainly in the western Mediterranean. Novorossiysk is a major port for exporting crude oil. The Caspian pipeline connects to several oilfields in Kazakhstan including the Tengiz oilfield, one of the largest oilfields in the world, to Novorossiysk. At the time, the *Aegean Horizon* was a relatively new vessel, having been built in the Hyundai Heavy Industries shipyard in Ulsan, South Korea, in 2007 for Leadership Shipping Inc of Monrovia, Liberia. As can be seen from her hull, she is operated and managed by Arcadia Shipmanagement of Athens and flies the flag of Greece.

(Chris Brooks)

The general cargo vessel **Afamia** passes Kandilli, as she makes her way northwards on 5 June 2008. She is bound for Odessa having started her voyage in ballast from Tartous, Syria. One of a large class of "TD15 type" of general cargo ships, she was built for Spanish owners in 1979 at the Astilleros Espanoles shipyard in Bilbao, Spain, as the **Karen S.**. She carried this name for just three years. A string of name changes followed – **Mikarenos** in 1982 retaining the Spanish flag, **Carolina Express** in 1986, **Maestro** in 1988, **Estro** in 1991 and back to **Maestro** in 1991, all under the Panamanian flag. In 1992 she became the Cypriot-flagged **Larak**. She kept this name until 2000 when she became the **Heng Shun**, flying the flag of Hong Kong. She finally became the **Afamia** in 2004, initially flying the flag of Dominica, and later Georgia. At the time of the photograph she was flying the Georgian flag, but a few months later transferred to that of Sierra Leone. Under the name **Afamia**, she has traded mainly between ports in the Black Sea and eastern Mediterranean since her sale to her current owners, the Deep Shipping Corporation, in 2004. Her commercial operators are the ISM Group of Beirut.

(Chris Brooks)

The veteran general cargo ship **Ahora** heads north past Kandilli on 6 October 2007 on passage from Ashdod to Odessa. She was delivered by Rauma-Repola Oy to Finska Angfartygs AB (Finland Steamship Company Ltd) in 1963 as **Argo**. Official records indicate that in 1970 she was lengthened, her length overall increasing from 116,4 to 130,99 metres. In 1981 she took the name **Leenor** for Israeli flag interests Yanor Marine Services Ltd. Her current name was adopted in 1989 when her registered owner became Vestview Shipping NV, of Curaçao, and she was placed under the Netherlands Antilles flag. As **Ahora**, apart from occasional visits to other Mediterranean ports, she has traded between Black Sea ports and Israel. After arriving at Bourgas in November 2008 a period of inactivity followed. In June 2009 she was transferred to the Georgian flag. Soon after following a Port State Control inspection she was detained for ten days with 26 reported deficiencies. The inspection record listed her owners as Argo Coral Maritime (Israel) Ltd, of Haifa, and gave the class society as the Indian Register of Shipping. She resumed trading in September 2009.

(Simon Smith)

The St Vincent & the Grenadines-flagged general cargo ship **Anastasia V** was on a northbound passage of the Bosphorus when passing Kandilli on 6 October 2007. She is a product of the Amels Shipyard at Makkum in the Netherlands and was delivered as **Passaat Brasil** in 1976, a name she was to maintain until 1984 when she became **Louise**. Further changes of ownership and name were to follow on a regular basis; **Lady Anthoula** in 1989, **Sea Wind** in 1998, **Sony K** in 2003, **Fayez T** in 2004, and **Frigate** in 2005, before becoming **Anastasia V** in May 2007. Her final name change took place in October 2008 when she became **Elisa Z**, after which ensued a traumatic period resulting in her total loss in July 2009. In late January 2009 she dragged anchor off Antalya, suffering damage to her propeller and rudder. In May 2009 she grounded again having dragged anchor off Dikili. Sadly, an unsuccessful refloating operation resulted in the subsequent death of a local fisherman after ropes parted. On 17 July whilst off the Turkish Black Sea coast on passage from Batumi to Istanbul with a cargo of iron she broadcast a distress signal. Shortly afterwards the crew, who were all rescued, abandoned the vessel and she sank in deep water.

(Simon Smith)

Heading northwards past Kandilli on passage from Thessalonika to Illichivsk on 6 October 2007 is the Fortune-type bulk carrier **Athlos**. The Japanese builder Ishikawajima-Harima Heavy Industries (IHI) delivered more than fifty of this standard class bulk carrier from its various shipyards in Japan between 1971 and 1982. The design by Quebec-based GTR Campbell followed on from the earlier Freedom and Freedom MkII general cargo vessels. In January 2010 only nine Fortunes survived. **Nin** was delivered to the Yugoslavian operator Tankerska Plovidba by IHI's Yokohama yard in 1978. She was sold to the Greek company Tide Line (registered owner Athlos Shipping Co.) at the turn of century and renamed **Athlos**. A further change of ownership was recorded in 2006 with sale to Golden Ship Maritime Co Ltd. She retained the name **Athlos** and her Maltese registry until 2009 when a further sale to Dubai-based Allami Shipping Services saw a name change to **Green Line** under the Panama flag. She currently trades between Karachi and Iraq carrying cement.

(Simon Smith)

The Belize-flagged bulk carrier **Belmopan** passes Kandilli on her northbound Bosphorus passage from Antalya to Mariupol on 13 August 2009. She is one of seven gearless handysize bulk carriers built for the Polish Steamship Company (Polska Zegluga Morska) by Neue Schlichting Werft GmbH at Travemünde between 1974 and 1976. **Huta Zygmunt** was the last of the series and was delivered to the Polish Steamship Company in 1976. She remained under the Polish flag until 2001 when she took her current name for the Turkish operator International Shipping Group and Trading Ltd. After spells under the flags of Panama and Cambodia she was registered in Belize City in 2004. The same company also operates the **Corozal**, another of the type that was delivered to PZM as **Kopalnia Walbrzych**. Only one vessel, the **Svatoy Nikolay** (delivered as **Budowlany**) has gone for demolition arriving at Alang in February 2009. Four of the class are trading for Riamar Shipping of Syria. The **Captain Eglio** (ex-**Kopalnia Sosnowiec**) and the **Captain Bashar** (ex-**Kopalnia Zofiowka**) joined Riamar in 2006 followed by **Captain Abdullah** (ex-**Huta Zgoda**) in 2007 and **Roln** (ex **Rolnik**) in 2010.

(Simon Smith)

On 28 June 2006 the Japanese-built general cargo ship **Captain Mustafa** passes close to the Asian side of the Bosphorus whilst sailing from Alexandria to Novorossiysk. She was completed by the Minami-Nippon Shipbuilding Co Ltd at Usuki in Japan's Oita Prefecture and is typical of many Japanese-built general cargo vessels dating from the 1970s engaged in Mediterranean and Black Sea trades. She began her career as **Yue Hope** following her completion in 1976. Her operator was listed as Pioneer Line Co Ltd (registered owner Bredia Shipholding SA). A 1989 sale to a Japanese owner saw her renamed **Artemis**. A further change of name to **Marygold** took place in the same year. In 1996 she was sold to Galatia Shipping Co SA of Piraeus taking the name **Captain Christos**. Her current name was adopted in 2001 following sale to Tartous-based Brilliant Marine SA (registered owners S and S Maritime Co Ltd). The sale also resulted in a transfer to the Cambodian flag. Since taking her current name **Captain Mustafa** has traded largely in the Black Sea and Mediterranean making over 140 Bosphorus transits. Occasional sorties elsewhere have taken her to India, Pakistan, West Africa and northern Europe. In December 2007 she was detained at Antwerp for nearly three months with an extensive list of deficiencies.

(Simon Smith)

The Panamanian-flagged **Cemrem** makes her way slowly up the Bosphorus on 3 June 2008. She is seen as she passes Kandilli, northbound, whilst on a voyage from Ashdod to Poti. The **Cemrem** dates from 1979 when she was completed at the AG Weser Seebeckwerft shipyard in Bremerhaven as **Laconikos**, for Greek owners. She changed her flag to that of Panama in 1982. In 1986 she passed to the Cypriot flag becoming the **Laconikos II**, subsequently taking the names **Laser Atlantic** in 1995, **Laconikos II** in 1998, **Nikos II** in 1999, **Sunrise R** in 2001 and **Rise** in 2003. In 2004 ownership passed to Mining Star Shipping Ltd of Malta, managed by Turkish interests, but flying the flag of Panama with the name **Lydia 1**. From February 2005 until April 2008, it seems she was employed on a regular trade between Güllük on the Mediterranean coast of Turkey and

Ravenna. Güllük is a small port situated in Bodrum Bay, engaged in the export of bauxite and feldspar. She was sold again in 2008 being subsequently operated by CMR Denizcilik ve Ticaret AS, of Istanbul, and renamed **Cemrem** under the flag of Panama. On 20 September 2009, she was reported at Port Louis, Mauritius, partially submerged with a flooded engine room and having been abandoned by her crew. She had been inactive and under arrest at Port Louis since 27 June 2009. Her cargo of rice was subsequently discharged and she was sold to shipbreakers, arriving at Alang under tow as the **Rem** on 16 February 2010. She was beached a few days later.

(Chris Brooks)

With Rumeli Hisarı castle in the background we see the general cargo vessel **Condor** passing Kandilli on 30 June 2006 whilst on voyage from Gemlik to Mariupol. Once a familiar sight in British waters, **Condor** was completed in 1970 by Hall, Russell & Co Ltd in Aberdeen, for Stephenson Clarke Shipping as **Malling**. She traded for Stephenson Clarke until 1991 when she was sold to Telmar Chartering Ltd (Torbulk Ltd) becoming **Torland**. She was sold to Paneldeal Ltd (Carisbrooke Shipping), of Cowes, in October 1992. Still trading as **Torland**, Carisbrooke sold her on even more quickly, passing to Greek owners in March 1993 as **Orlan**. At this point she took the flag of St Vincent & the Grenadines. In 1996 after a further change of ownership, she was sold to the Cihan Shipping Co Ltd of Istanbul as **Cihan** under the Maltese flag. Her final change of owners came in 2004, when she was sold to Conway Shipping Ltd of Malta, but still managed by Cihan Shipping. It was at this point that she gained her present name of **Condor**. Her flag was changed to that of the Cook Islands in August 2009. Under these owners, she initially traded between Turkish ports in the Sea of Marmara and the Ukraine. However, in April 2009, she crossed the Atlantic to start trading between Georgetown in Guyana, Kingston in Jamaica, and Suriname. She arrived in Bruges from Nieuw Nickerie, Suriname, on 20 April 2010 with a cargo of rice. Subsequently failing an inspection, she was abandoned by her owners and remains in Bruges at the time of writing.

(Chris Brooks)

The sisterships **Polar Costa Rica** and **Polar Honduras** were completed at Lübeck by Flender-Werke in 1979 for West German operator Hamburg-Süd. Since delivery the pair have followed similar career paths. In 1981 they were renamed **Caribbean Universal** and **Edinburgh Universal**, sailing under the Red Ensign for a time before adopting Sri Lankan registry in 1983. After a period as **Bering Universal** between 1989 and 1994 **Polar Costa Rica** reverted to her original name. **Polar Honduras** followed suit the same year having taken the name **Caspian Universal** in 1984 and **Caspian** in 1988. The names **Crystal Lily** and **Crystal Orchid** were acquired in September 2005 following sale to Russian interests. The sisters had been registered in Malta in 2003. At thirty years of age the inevitable followed with sale to Indian breakers, both vessels anchoring off Alang on 11 August 2009. **Crystal Lily** was beached ten days later with **Crystal Orchid** stopping engines for the last time the following day. She made a fine sight passing Kandilli northbound on 3 June 2008 whilst on passage from Tartous for Novorossiysk.

(Simon Smith)

The small livestock carrier **Falcon 1** heads northbound past Kandilli on 6 October 2007 on passage to Midia in Romania. She is one of many coasters built in Dutch and West German shipyards that have been converted into livestock carriers. **Falcon 1** is a product of Hamburg's prolific J J Sietas shipyard and was delivered to West German owners in 1965 as **Polaris**. In 1974 she became **Rien Teekman** for Dutch interests under Wagenborg management. A further change of ownership to Lebanese interests in 1977 saw her transferred to the Panama flag and renamed **Bianca W**. Movement reports suggest that she continued to trade in northern Europe under this name. She transferred to Lebanese registry in late 1980 taking the name **Al Salam III**. Her current name and Sierra Leone registry were acquired in 2007. Official sources do not record when conversion to a livestock carrier took place. Since 2007 she has made a number of Bosphorus passages sailing northbound in ballast for Romania or Georgia and returning southbound with her live cargo, usually for Beirut or Tartous.

(Simon Smith)

In perfect lighting conditions for photography, the **Green Nova** passes Kandilli on 4 June 2008, whilst on a voyage from Houston, Texas to Mariupol in the Ukraine. **Green Nova** was built in 1992 at the Kitanihon Shipbuilding Co Ltd at Hachinohe, Japan, as **Nova Klipper**. Her owners at this time were the NV Shipping Co Nova Klipper, a company registered in the Netherlands Antilles. She was part of the fleet of vessels managed by Seatrade Groningen. She remained as **Nova Klipper** until early 2007, when she was sold to Green Shipping AS of Norway and renamed **Green Nova**, being operated by Green Reefers ASA of Norway. At this time she took the flag of the Bahamas.

(Chris Brooks)

Occasionally the Bosphorus provides the ship photographer with a mystery vessel. At first glance this is a typical small Turkish coaster, but she possibly hides an interesting history. According to various publications, *Hantallar* was built in 1906 by Earle's Shipbuilding and Engineering Co Ltd, of Hull, as *Cleopatra*. She was a fishing vessel built for Hellyer's Fishing, of Grimsby, who operated a large fleet of fishing vessels in the North Sea. She sailed with Hellyer's until the First World War, when she was requisitioned as a minesweeper. She was sold on 16 April 1919 and her Hull fishing registry was closed on 31 July of that year when it was noted that she was no longer employed in fishing. She was listed as a salvage ship in the London Ship Register of 1920. By the early 1930s she had passed to Turkish ownership and she took the name

Kleopatra in 1933 and then *Kilyos* in 1935. In the late 1960s she was sold to K. Soltoglu of Turkey and renamed *Sadik Kaptan*. At this point, it appears she was lengthened, re-engined and converted to a general cargo ship. She retained the name *Sadik Kaptan* until 1982, when she was sold to R. Hantal of Eregli, Turkey, taking the name *Hantallar*. Whether or not the *Hantallar* is actually based on the 1906 vessel remains to be seen, for it is obvious that little remains of the original vessel. *Hantallar* is regularly seen plodding up and down the Bosphorus as she trades between Turkish ports in the Sea of Marmara and ports on the Black Sea coast of Turkey. She is seen passing Kandilli northbound on 8 October 2008.

(Chris Brooks)

Typical of the modern vessels being built locally at Tuzla is the general cargo ship *Hikmet K.* She was built at the Gisan Gemi Insa Sanayi shipyard at Tuzla, having been laid down in September 2002 and handed over to her new owners at the end of January 2004. Since completion she has been owned by Irem Denizcilik, a local company based in Istanbul, currently owning two ships. Management of the vessel is in the hands of Simge Denizcilik ve Ticaret AS, also a local Istanbul-based company. At the time of the photograph, taken on 5 June 2008, she was on a voyage from Diliskelesi, in the Sea of Marmara, bound for the Black Sea. She is a familiar sight in the Bosphorus as she trades between Black Sea ports and Turkish ports in the Sea of Marmara with occasional visits to several countries in the Mediterranean.

(Chris Brooks)

The **Iran Sarbaz** catches a last glimpse of sunshine as she passes Kandilli, northbound, before heavy rain hits the Bosphorus on 10 October 2008. At the time she was on a voyage from Aqaba in Jordan via the Suez Canal to Nikolayev in the Ukraine in ballast. She returned from the Black Sea, passing through the Bosphorus, southbound on 2 November 2008 after loading cargo in Nikolayev, bound for the Suez Canal. **Iran Sarbaz** was built in 1984 at the Izar Shipyard at Seville, Spain for the Islamic Republic of Iran Shipping Lines (IRISL) of Tehran. Unusually, after almost 25 years of trade, she remained in service with her original owners, with no name changes. Six months after the photograph was taken she was laid up at Bandar Abbas and finally found her way to Alang where she was beached in September 2010. Two other vessels of the same class were built at the same time for the company. The **Iran Akhavan** was completed in 1984. She was reported sold to breakers in November 2009 having taken the name **Ruby K** but was reprieved and currently trades as the North Korean-flagged **Gem 1**. The third of the trio, **Iran Amanat**, was completed in 1983. She was renamed **Tabak** by the company in late 2008 and remains in service.

(Chris Brooks)

Seen approaching Kandilli on 14 July 2007 is the **Kavarna**. This vessel dates from 1982 when she was completed at the "Ivan Dimitrov" Shipyard at Rousse, a city in Bulgaria, situated on the banks of the River Danube, 200 kilometres away from the Black Sea coast. This vessel is immediately recognisable as one of the large Sormovskiy class of sea/river ships. She is one of nine of this class of vessel which were built at Rousse during the early 1980s. At the time of the photograph, she was owned by Navigation Maritime Bulgare (NAVIBULGAR), the successor to the state-owned shipping company from the Communist era and had been with this company since completion in 1982. During 2009 she was sold by NAVIBULGAR to Asta Trading and Shipping Ltd of Panama. Management was passed to the Istanbul-based company Yagmur Deniz Tasımacılıgı Ticaret Ltd Sirketi. Her new owners renamed her **Galisa** and she now flies the flag of Moldova. **Kavarna** was on a voyage from Alexandria and El Dekheila in Egypt to Constantza in Romania when photographed. This is a typical example of her trading pattern over the last few years.

(Chris Brooks)

The **Kumdas 2** is typical of the local coastal vessels that traverse the Bosphorus daily. Since her sale to her current owners in 2006 she appears to have traded exclusively between Turkish Black Sea ports and ports in the Sea of Marmara, hence she is a common sight in the Bosphorus. She is seen passing northbound at Kandilli on 6 June 2008. The **Kumdas 2** dates from 1974 when she was completed at the Gemi-is Kollektif shipyard in Istanbul. Launched as the **Sadan Kaptanoglu**, she retained this name until 1991 when she was sold by her original owners to Fahri Eksioglu & Mehmet Eksioglu of Istanbul and renamed **Fahri Eksioglu II**. She remained with this company until 2006 when she was sold to another company, Kumdas Denizcilik Insaat Malzemeleri Tasımacılık ve Ticaret AS, again, a local company based in Kartal, near Istanbul. Upon purchase by this company, she joined her smaller fleetmate the **Kumdas**, which was purchased by the company in 2005, and renamed **Kumdas 2**.

(Chris Brooks)

The distinctive funnel colours are a clue to the origins of this veteran general cargo ship. She was built in 1969 at the VEB Schiffswerft Neptun Shipyard in Rostock, East Germany, as the *Bruni*, a name she retained only until 1974. In this year she became the *Fredericksgate* owned by Hull Gates Shipping Co Ltd, flying the British flag. In 1975 she became the *Eskdalegate*, again under the British flag and operated by Turnbull Scott Management Ltd. She remained under this name until 1977 when she was renamed *Elisabeth* having been purchased by Cancyp Maritime Ltd of Cyprus, but operated by Helmsing and Grimm, of Hamburg. She flew the flag of Cyprus at this time. She remained with Helmsing and Grimm for 27 years until 2004 when she was sold.

Initially renamed *Staropoliye*, this changed after a few months when she was sold to Lisa Shipping Inc of Batumi, Georgia, and renamed *Lisa*, flying the flag of Georgia. In 2007 her flag changed to that of Comoros. She is currently managed by CK Shipping & Trading Ltd, of Istanbul, with Lisa Shipping Inc remaining her owners. Her funnel colours are little changed from her days with Helmsing and Grimm, only a small red insignia has been added to her original colours. The *Lisa* was photographed passing northwards through the Bosphorus at Kandilli on 9 August 2009. At the time, she was on a voyage from the Turkish port of Eregli, situated in the Sea of Marmara, to Constantza, and has regularly traded between these two ports since May 2007.

(Chris Brooks)

The general cargo ship **Mega Star** passes Kandilli, northbound on 6 June 2008. She had previously departed from Damietta, Egypt on 2 June and was bound for Nikolayev. Since May 2006, she has traded almost exclusively between ports in Ukraine and Syria, Egypt, Tunisia and Libya. She was built in 1979 at the Kanasashi Zosen shipyard in Toyohashi, Japan. Her owner at that time was the Algerian state-owned shipping company, Société Nationale de Transportes Maritimes & Compagnie Nationale Algérienne de Navigation (SNTM–CNAN) and she carried the name of **Bel-Abbes**. She was one of four sisters built for the company, the others being the **Bechar**, **Biskra** and **Bouira**. **Bel-Abbes** remained with SNTM-CNAN until 2006 when she was sold to Mega Star Shipping Ltd of Alexandria and renamed **Mega Star**. At that point her flag was changed from that of Algeria to St Vincent & the Grenadines. Although owned by that company, she was managed by the National Shipping and Investment Co of Alexandria. Ownership passed to the National Shipping and Investment Co later in 2006. Since April 2010 she has flown the flag of Tanzania having been sold to Syrian interests. Her sisterships had mixed careers, the **Bechar** sank off Algeria on 13 November 2004 with the loss of 18 crew members. The **Biskra** was broken up at Alang as the **Iskra** in 2004. The **Bouira** was broken up at Mumbai as **Princess Layan** in 2009. This leaves the **Mega Star** as the sole survivor of her class.

(Chris Brooks)

Seen passing Kandilli on 6 October 2007, **Mikhail Stenko** was one of a rapidly diminishing class of Soviet-built vessels. Between 1972 and 1978 the Vyborg shipyard produced fourteen of the "Nikolay Zhukov" class. They are slightly larger than the "Pioner Moskvy" type which were built at the same yard and will be more familiar to readers in northern Europe. Twelve of the class were delivered to Soviet Union owners, including six to the Black Sea Shipping Co, three to the Kamchatka Shipping Co and three to the Azov Shipping Co. The remaining two went to Singapore flag interests. Although during her thirty-four year career she traded under five flags (Soviet Union, Russia, Ukraine,

Honduras and Georgia), she bore only two names, trading as **Mikhail Stenko**, except for a period between 2001 and 2003 when she operated as **Sea Mirage**. When photographed she flew the Ukrainian flag and was registered in Mariupol for owners Commercial Fleet, of Donbass. Apart from one vessel that was lost in the South China Sea, the class all traded into the twenty-first century. By the end of 2010 only three vessels remained. **Mikhail Stenko** passed Istanbul for the last time on 3 March 2009. She was beached at Alang some six weeks later.

(Simon Smith)

54

The vessels of the Bulgarian Navigation Maritime Bulgare (NAVIBULGAR) are a regular sight in the Bosphorus, as one would expect with Bulgaria's only ports situated within the Black Sea. A large number of bulk carriers are owned and operated by this company and one of these was seen passing Kandilli on 4 June 2008. *Musala* was on a voyage from Gebze in the Sea of Marmara, to the Russian Black Sea port of Tuapse. A product of the Hitachi Zosen shipyard at Innoshima, Japan, she was completed in 1967 and has remained with NAVIBULGAR throughout her long life. One of seven sisters completed between 1967 and 1968, with *Murgash*, *Ruen* and *Vejen* being completed at Innoshima. The remaining three, *Buzludja*, *Ludogoretz* and *Oborishte* were built at Setoda Zosen, in Setoda, Japan. Not long after this photograph was taken the *Musala* arrived at her home port of Varna on 24 October 2008. Here she remained inactive and under repair. One must assume that the repairs were not successful, or at least only temporary, as she departed from Varna on 22 May 2009, bound for Aliaga. She subsequently arrived at Aliaga on 30 May for breaking. Of her sisters, *Buzludja*, *Oborishte* and *Ruen* were broken up at Aliaga in 2009. *Murgash* found her way to Gadani Beach, Pakistan, for breaking also in 2009. *Ludogoretz* (renamed *Ludo*) arrived at Alang late in 2010. The *Vejen* (renamed *Teteven* in 2008) appears to have been inactive in Varna for most of 2010 and is the sole survivor of the class.

(Chris Brooks)

The general cargo vessel **Naftobulk III** began her life in the China Shipbuilding Corporation's shipyard in Kaohsiung, Taiwan in 1979. Initially named **Chiang Wei** under the Liberian flag, she carried this name for only two years, becoming **Asian Diamond** in 1981, **Pacific Diamond** in 1982 and **Asian Argosy** in 1985. During these name changes she continued to fly the flag of Liberia. In 1987 she was sold to Splitska Plovidba dd of Split in Croatia, a company associated with the Government of Yugoslavia who were her beneficial owners. At this point she was renamed **Sutla**, a name she carried for ten years. Although classed as a general cargo ship, it seems at that time she was involved in the carriage of cement. For a short time in 1992, she was owned by the Cement Transport & Shipping Co Ltd of Liberia. She was renamed **Argyro M** in 1997 under the Cypriot flag. In 2004 she was sold to the Steel Securities Group Inc of Panama, and renamed **Naftobulk III** under the St Vincent & the Grenadines flag. Her managers were the Naftotrade Shipping & Commercial Co SA of Piraeus, a company that specialises in the carriage of cement by sea and consequently operates a large fleet of specialised cement carriers. At the time of this photograph, taken on 10 October 2008, she was passing Kandilli, northbound, whilst on a voyage from Derince, Turkey, to Nikolayev in the Ukraine. She traded for a further two years, being sold to breakers in December 2010.

(Chris Brooks)

The **Odisk**, recognisable as a member of the "STK" type of Russian sea-river vessel, was completed as the **Om** in 1980 at the VEB Elbewerften shipyard at Rosslau, Germany. She was owned by the Irtysh River Shipping Co, of Russia, until 2003 when she was acquired by Albros Shipping and Trading, of Istanbul, and renamed **Modisk 6**. In July 2005 her name was shortened to **Odisk**, but she remained within the Albros Group. Her flag at that time was changed from Russia to Georgia. It is under the Albros Group ownership that we see her passing Kandilli, northbound, on 30 June 2006 whilst on a voyage from Eleusis. On 6 January 2007 during a voyage from Kerch to Iskenderun, with a cargo of ferro-silico manganese, two of her crew members died due to poisoning from chemicals released from the cargo. The remainder of the crew were also hospitalised. She was subsequently towed back to Kerch where her cargo was unloaded, and remained at Kerch detained until April 2007. After this incident, the Albros Group disposed of her in May 2007 to Yildirim Shipping SA when she was renamed **Aras 10**. Under this ownership she was managed by an Istanbul-based company. She was subsequently renamed **Yildirimlar-1** in May 2008 and remains in service with Yildirim Shipping SA, flying the flag of Sierra Leone.

(Chris Brooks)

A product of the Santierul Naval Galati shipyard at Galatz, Romania, the bulk carrier **Oasis West** was built as the **Tirgu Lapus** in 1978. She was one of eight "Pionierul" type vessels built between 1977 and 1979 at Galatz. She initially entered service with Navrom of Romania and remained with them until ownership passed to Compania de Navigatie Maritime PETROMIN SA of Constantza in the early 1990s. She remained under this ownership until 2005, having been renamed **Tania** in 2001 and **Talia S** in 2003. In 2005 she was sold by her Romanian owners to Oasis Shipping & Trading Ltd of Panama and renamed **Oasis West**, her managers being based in Izmir, Turkey. Initially flagged in Panama, in August 2008 she was reflagged to the republic of Moldova, with registry being in the port of Giurgiulesti, a port on the River Danube. Photographed on 8 October 2008 passing Kandili northbound, she was on a voyage from Ravenna to Eregli, a port situated on Turkey's Black Sea coast. In fact, she has traded almost exclusively between Italian and Turkish ports since her sale to her new owners in 2005. Four of her sisterships were scrapped in 1999, including the name ship of the class the **Pionierul**. She was one of three broken up at Aliaga in that year, the others being **Tirgu Bujor** and **Tirgu Ocna**. **Tirgu Trotus** found her way to Indian breakers at Kolkata, having been renamed **Orama 1**. In November 2010, **Oasis West** was noted off Pakistan bound for Gadani Beach.

(Chris Brooks)

Vessels of this type are becoming increasingly rare, even in the Bosphorus. The **Rama H** dates from 1975, being completed as the **Komsomolets Turkmenii** at the "A Zhdanov" shipyard in Leningrad. She was one of the last of a class of some 37 ships built at this shipyard between 1968 and 1975. It is believed that the **Rama H** is the last of this class of vessel still in existence. A series of nine similar vessels were built in Alexandria, for local owners. A handful of these remain in service. The **Komsomolets Turkmenii** was fitted initially with three 8-tonne cranes, four 5-tonne derricks and a single 40-tonne derrick. The earlier units of the class were fitted with five 8-tonne cranes only. At some point in her career, her derricks have been removed. **Komsomolets Turkmenii** remained under the flags of USSR, and later Russia, operated by the Far Eastern Shipping Co (FESCO) until 1996. In this year she was sold to Evergreen Ltd of Malta and renamed **Sinjar** and then renamed **Celmera K** in December 1996. At this time she was managed by I M Marine Services (London) Ltd. In 2007 she was again sold, this time to Black Sea Marine, a company based in Syria, her managers being the Arados Shipping Co Srl of Constantza, Romania. Upon this ownership change, she received her current name **Rama H** flying the flag of Georgia. She currently trades between the Black Sea and the eastern Mediterranean - in particular, ports in Egypt, Syria and the Lebanon. It is on such a voyage that we see her passing Kandilli northbound whilst on a voyage from Damietta to Kerch on 9 August 2009.

(Chris Brooks)

With less than a year of her career remaining, the containership ***Rialto*** heads north past Kandilli en-route to Odessa on 1 June 2008. She was one of a pair of 574 TEU vessels produced by the Hamburg builder J J Sietas in 1977 for the Yugoslavian government-owned operator Jugolinija. She was delivered as ***Susak*** and named after a suburb of Rijeka. In 1992 Jugolinija became Croatia Line and ***Susak*** joined the Croatian register in 1996. In 2002 ***Susak*** was sold to UK flag interests G & O Shipping (UK) Ltd and became ***Claudia A***. A further sale followed two years later when she became ***Rialto*** for

Athens-based Sarlis Group under the Panamanian flag. Meanwhile sistership ***Hrelijn*** had been renamed ***Mayzunah*** in 1992, before reverting to ***Hreljin*** a year later. She also passed into G & O Shipping ownership as ***Carolina A*** in 2001, before arriving at Alang for demolition in 2003. ***Rialto*** passed south through the Suez Canal on 14 February 2009 and anchored off Mumbai ten days later. She was beached on 3 March with demolition commencing eleven days later.

(Simon Smith)

The bulk carrier **Sami Canbaz** passes very close to Kandilli on 15 August 2009, so close that she almost washed the photographer into the Bosphorus! She is one of a large class of vessels built at Shanghai by the Jiangnan Shipyard between 1975 and 1992 and began life as **Hong Qi 205**. Many of the vessels have served China Shipping throughout their careers operating in the coal trades between northern China and major cities further south, such as Shanghai. A number of the ships were sold to European owners, some of which have since returned to the Chinese flag. Four vessels were acquired by the Greek company Pacific & Atlantic Corp. in 1997, trading as **Bulk Amethyst**, **Bulk Diamond**, **Bulk Emerald** and **Bulk Sapphire**. Two of the quartet have since returned to China.

Bulk Sapphire became **Lady Mafra** in 2004 before she was sold to Turkish owners in 2007 and renamed **Gozde D**. The **Bulk Emerald** became **Maya B** in 2003 before she too passed to Turkish owners in 2007 as **H. Necat Sagbas**. Later in the same year she became **Sami Canbaz** for Canbaz Shipping & Transport. On 9 October 2009 **Sami Canbaz** suffered an explosion and subsequent engine room fire whilst on passage from Illichevsk to Ashdod with a cargo of scrap iron. Two days later she arrived off Famagusta in tow of the tug **Sonduren 7**. She continues to trade in the Black Sea having transferred to the Moldovan flag in early 2010.

(Simon Smith)

The **Sea Omar** dates from 1965, when she was completed as the **Friesland**. Built at the Schlichting-Werft shipyard at Travemünde, she spent her early career in the fleet of Peter Döhle Schiffahrts, of Hamburg. In 1990 she passed to the Carolina Cia Nav SA being renamed **Ioanna**, flying the Honduran flag. In 1999 she was sold to World Glory SA, transferring to the flag of Panama but she retained her name. The year 2004 saw her sold to M Othman, a company registered in North Korea, and renamed **Iman A**. Sold again in 2005, she retained her North Korean flag, but was renamed **Sea Omar**. In 2007 she was sold to the United Transport Co of Syria under the Cambodian flag, being managed by the Khaled Maritime Co of Tartous, Syria. Here we see the **Sea Omar** passing Kandilli on 11 July 2007, northbound, whilst on a voyage from Abu Kir, Egypt, for Novorossiysk. On arrival at Novorossiysk she was subsequently detained with a long list of deficiencies until 26 July 2007. In March 2010 she grounded off Platiyali, Greece. Subsequently refloated, she was towed into port, arrested and detained there for an extended period. Late in 2010 she arrived off Aliaga, presumably for demolition.

(Chris Brooks)

Immediately recognisable as a product of the J J Sietas shipyard at Hamburg, the **Snow White** will also be a familiar vessel to many northern European ship enthusiasts. This vessel had previously traded to northern Europe until July 2007 when she departed for the eastern Mediterranean under her new name. **Snow White** was originally completed in 1975 for the Compagnie Marocaine de Navigation (COMANAV) of Morocco as the **Ouirgane**. She had two identical sisters, both completed in 1975 for the same company, the **Ouezzane** and **Ouarzazate**. Two later, similar ships the **Oulmes** and **Oualidia** were also delivered in 1978. The **Ouirgane** maintained a regular service between Morocco, Spain, Portugal and northern Europe and was with this company for some 27 years before being sold. In 2002 she was purchased by Abnett Overseas Corporation and renamed **Abnett Snow**, her flag being changed to that of Cambodia. For the next five years she traded for that company, predominantly between St. Petersburg and northern European ports, mainly in the Netherlands. In 2007 she passed to the Eldora Shipping Co and received her current name, flying the flag of Sierra Leone. Since that time she has traded between ports in the eastern Mediterranean and Black Sea. She is seen passing Kandili northbound in the early morning autumn sunshine, whilst on a voyage from Mudanya, a small Turkish port on the southern coast of the Sea of Marmara, to Constantza on 7 October 2008.

(Chris Brooks)

The bulk carrier **Stelios B** makes an impressive sight as she sails past Kandilli on the morning of 14 August 2009 in excellent photographic conditions. She was on a voyage from Piraeus to Odessa. The **Stelios B** was built in 1985 at the Hyundai Heavy Industries yard at Ulsan, South Korea. She was completed as **Wadi Al Nakheel** for the National Navigation Co, of Egypt, a company set up in the early 1980s, with assistance from the Egyptian government. The company specialised in the drybulk trades and as such, she was one of four sisterships ordered by the company from the Hyundai shipyard at Ulsan

in the mid-1980s. Two of the four sisters were sold in 2000 to single vessel companies associated with A. B. Maritime Inc, of Piraeus. **Wadi Al Natroon** became **Spyros B** whilst **Wadi Al Nakheel** became **Stelios B**. Initially, on their sale they flew the flag of Greece, but that was changed to the Maltese flag in 2004. The remaining two sisterships, **Wadi Al Kamar** and **Wadi Al Molouk**, remained in the company for a few more years being sold to the Guangzhou Pan Ocean Shipping Co, of China, being renamed **Yue Xiu Hai** and **Hua Du Hai** respectively.

(Chris Brooks)

Cruise ships frequently travel through the Bosphorus. The veteran cruise ship **The Emerald** passes Kandilli on 8 October 2008, on a voyage from Kusadası to Odessa. **The Emerald** was built in 1958 at the Newport News Shipyard in the USA as the general cargo and passenger ship **Santa Rosa** for Grace Line. This company was engaged in passenger and cargo trade between North America, Central America and the Caribbean. **Santa Rosa** and her sistership **Santa Paula** served in this trade until 1970 when Grace Line was purchased by Prudential Line. Subsequently laid up, the **Santa Rosa** remained laid up for 18 years, before she was acquired by Coral Cruise Lines. She was towed to Greece, where she was converted to a cruise ship in 1992, as the **Diamond Island**.

In late 1992 she emerged from her conversion, much changed in appearance as the **Regent Rainbow** of Regency Cruises. She remained with Regency Cruises until that company went bankrupt in 1995. Sold to Louis Cruises of Cyprus after the demise of Regency, she continues with that company to this day. Although operated by Louis Cruises, she spent some time on charter to Thomson Cruises whose colours the vessel was wearing in the photograph. This charter ended in November 2008, and she was returned to Louis. Following several months of lay-up at Eleusis, Louis operated her during 2009. It was unclear what the future held for this fine vessel as the time approached for the implementation of the Solas 2010 regulations.

(Chris Brooks)

The **Tokay Çillioglu**, riding high in the water at a somewhat precarious angle was seen passing Kandilli, northbound, whilst on a voyage from Derince to Mariupol on 5 June 2008. She is a former member of the Dutch Spliethoff fleet of vessels, being built in common with many other Spliethoff vessels at the Miho Zosensho Shipyard at Shimizu, Japan in 1978. Initially, she was completed as **Westaftrader** flying the flag of Panama, but passed into the fleet of Spliethoff in 1981 as **Snoekgracht**. She remained with Spliethoff, flying the Dutch flag until 1993 when she was sold to Salpoort Shipping NV of the Netherlands Antilles. She was renamed **Leuvehaven** and a year later **Tropical Carrier** and operated by Van Uden Group BV of the Netherlands. She subsequently carried the names **Fiducia**, **President** and **Roubini II**, flying the Netherlands Antilles,

Italian and Liberian flags respectively between 1995 and 2007. Her present owners, Çillioglu Denizcilik Nakliyat of Istanbul acquired her in 2007 and renamed her **Tokay Çillioglu**. On 28 September 2008, **Tokay Çillioglu** ran into trouble in the Black Sea, on a voyage from Theodosia to Bandirma with a cargo of clay. About 20 miles off the northern entrance to the Bosphorus in heavy weather, she requested assistance, and was escorted into Istanbul anchorage by a tug. She remained in the anchorage until 16 November when she resumed her voyage to Bandirma. There have been no reported movements for her since July 2009 and she is currently laid up in Tuzla anchorage.

(Chris Brooks)

The **Yeni Gül Kardesler-II** is typical of the small coasters that ply their trade up and down the Bosphorus. She trades between ports in the Sea of Marmara and Turkish ports in the Black Sea, with occasional visits to Constantza in Romania. Although the name of this vessel appears on the hull as **Yenigül Kardesler II**, she is listed in most publications as the **Yeni Gül Kardesler-II**. **Yeni Gül Kardesler-II** was built in 1967, in the local shipyard of Denizcilik Anonim Sirketi Beykoz Tersanesi at Beykoz, a suburb on the Asian side of the Bosphorus. Originally completed as the **Haldun**, she retained this name until 1990 when she was renamed **Alipasa-4**. She traded as the **Alipasa-4** for just over ten years before taking the name **Yeni Gül Kardesler II** in 2000. Her owners are currently listed as Mehmet ve Celal Gül Abdullah, of Üsküdar, Istanbul.

(Chris Brooks)

The cruise ferry **Yuzhnaya Palmyra** is seen passing Kandilli on 14 August 2009 on a voyage from Istanbul to Odessa. At that time she maintained a service offering regular cruises from Odessa to Istanbul for the ZAO Ukrferry Shipping Co of Odessa. Occasional cruises were also undertaken from Odessa to Yalta. This proved to be her last year on the service, being withdrawn at the end of the summer season. She was replaced by Ukrferry's smaller **Caledonia** until the service was withdrawn in July 2010. The **Yuzhnaya Palmyra**, began life as the **Silesia** when she was built in 1979 at Stocznia Szczecinska im A Warskiego at Szczecin, Poland, for Polferries (Polish Baltic Shipping Co). She was the second of the "B490" type built at the shipyard, the first being the **Pomerania**, also built for Polferries in 1978. Two more of the type were also built for Turkish Maritime Lines. The **Ankara**, was completed in 1983 and the **Samsun** in 1985. **Silesia** remained with Polferries until 2005, when she was sold to GA Ferries of Greece and renamed **Felicia**. She was quickly sold on, this time to the Asteron Trade Corporation of Panama, her present owners. At this point she joined the Ukrferry fleet as the **Yuzhnaya Palmyra** in March 2006. From May 2008 until January 2009 the **Yuzhnaya Palmyra** was chartered to Spain's ISCOMAR to run a service linking Denia with Ibiza. Renamed **Begona Del Mar**, she received a yellow livery, the remnants of which are evident in this photograph. Following her withdrawal, she remains laid up and is believed to be inactive at Illichivsk late in 2010.

(Chris Brooks)

In the afternoon, a southbound convoy normally operates in the Bosphorus. An ideal location from which to photograph the southbound convoy is on the European side of the waterway, near the ancient fortress of Rumeli Hisarı. Passing Rumeli Hisarı on 10 August 2009 is the bulk carrier *Al Naser*. When photographed, she was on a voyage from Bartın, on the Black Sea coast of Turkey, to Alexandria. *Al Naser* began life as the *Clivia* at the Watanabe Zosen shipyard at Hakata, Japan, in 1977. Initially, she was owned by Clivia Schiffahrtsgesellschaft mbH & Co KG of Bremen, Germany, and managed by Herm Dauelsberg GmbH & Co KG, also based in Bremen. She flew the German flag and stayed with her owners for less than two years. She was renamed *Olinda* in 1978, passing to Mistral Shipping and Trading Pte Ltd flying the Singapore flag. In 1990 she reverted to *Clivia* and her original owners and managers, but this time, was flagged in Liberia. During 1995 she was renamed *Nicola D* when she was purchased by the Nicola D Shipping Co Ltd, of Cyprus, being managed by Dobson Lines, also of Cyprus. She remained under the Dobson Lines management until 2005 when she was again sold, this time to Zahra Maritime Services Co of Tartous, Syria. Under her new owners she was renamed *Al Naser* and flagged in Georgia. Since 2005, she has traded between ports in the Black Sea and ports in Syria, Egypt, Libya and Algeria.

(Chris Brooks)

The refrigerated cargo ship **Crystal Hope** dates from 1975, when she was built by the Shikoku Dockyard Co Ltd at Takamatsu, Japan. Completed as the **Rose Acacia**, flying the flag of Panama, she bore this name for only three years, becoming the **White Jasmin** in 1978. She retained this name, again under the Panamanian flag until 1989, when she was sold to Oriental Liberty SA of Panama becoming the **Ionian Sprinter**. In 1996 she became the property of the Gulfstream Shipping Corp, of Athens, changing her name to **Crystal Hope** under the St Vincent & the Grenadines flag, remaining with this company for almost ten years. In 2005 she was again sold to Sia Firma Baltkraft, of Latvia, but retained the name of **Crystal Hope** and her St Vincent & the Grenadines flag. Although owned by a Latvian company, she is operated by UAB Alliance Marine of Lithuania. She was under this ownership when she was photographed on 31 May 2008, passing Rumeli Hisarı, proceeding southwards in the Bosphorus, whilst on a voyage from Novorossiysk to Las Palmas. Early in 2010 she was again sold to Seafish Trade Ltd, of Lithuania, her managers remaining unchanged.

(Chris Brooks)

Late afternoon sunshine accompanies the Sietas-built coaster **Letfallah 4** as she passes Rumeli Hisarı on 12 August 2009. She was on passage from the Turkish Black Sea port of Bartin for Benghazi. The famous J J Sietas shipyard just outside Hamburg produced sixteen of the Type 67 design for German owners between 1970 and 1972. Some early examples were built without cranes but the majority including the **Letfallah 4** were equipped with two 12 to 15 tonne cranes. Depending on the crane configuration, the vessels had a container capacity of between 128 and 160 TEU. Delivered as **Baltica** in 1971, she became **Scol Hunter** in 1976 before reverting to **Baltica** in 1977. Leaving the West German flag for that of Colombia, she became **San Pancracio I** in 1984. Ten years later, she again reverted to **Baltica**, this time under the Honduran flag. A sale to Syrian interests in 2002 resulted in the name **Taha 1** and Cambodian registry. Her current name was acquired in 2009 for registered owners listed as Mariposa Maritime Inc. The Type 67 series has proved to be quite durable with only one vessel being delivered for demolition. Two vessels were lost in 1986 and a third foundered off South Africa in 2002. Apart from the **Serine** which remains under long-term arrest at Sibenik, the other ships continue to trade primarily in the Black Sea and Mediterranean areas.

(Simon Smith)

Kanlica, a small town on the Asian side of the Bosphorus, is located just to the north of the Fatih Mehmet Sultan Bridge. The town has a ferry terminal, which is served by the "Tourist Ferry". The St Vincent & the Grenadines-flagged general cargo vessel **Kourosh Pioneer** passes Kanlica northbound on 13 August 2009. She is the penultimate vessel of a class of twenty-four produced at Navashino between 1978 and 1989. **Nikolay Dolinskiy** was delivered to the Soviet Far Eastern Shipping Co in 1988. In 2006 she was sold to Moscow-based Sakhalinmortrans Ltd and renamed **Stalingrad**. Until 2008 she had traded exclusively in the Far East, but she passed northbound through the Suez Canal in February 2008, and continued to trade in northern Europe through the rest of the year arriving at Liverpool on 15 December. Her stay on Merseyside proved to be a lengthy one. According to the International Labour Organisation she was arrested by bunker suppliers in respect of unpaid debts. Her crew of fourteen were abandoned having not been paid for some months. She did not leave Liverpool until 5 April 2009, by which time she had been acquired by Turkish interests at auction and renamed **Kourosh Pioneer**. After leaving Liverpool she suffered further detentions at Lisbon and Ashdod. When photographed she was on passage from Tuzla for Odessa. Her smart appearance suggested that dry-docking had taken place at Tuzla.

(Simon Smith)

From Kanlica, it is possible to board the "Tourist Ferry" to the northern sections of the Bosphorus. On occasions it is possible that the ferry will coincide with the passing of a few vessels. In 2009 the sight of a large general cargo ship approaching her fortieth year is a rare event indeed. Fortune favoured the photographer on 14 August 2009 as the Cambodian-flagged *Baraka* made a northbound Bosphorus passage in daylight hours. At the time she was on passage from Damietta for Odessa in ballast. Launched in 1970 as *Chertal* she was one of four sisterships delivered to Belgian operator Bocimar by N.V. Boelwerf at Temse. Bocimar resulted from an arrangement between the Boel (founders of Boelwerf shipyard) and Cigrang families and was acquired by Companie Maritime Belge (CMB) in 1986. *Chertal* left the fleet in 1981 and was renamed *Antofagasta* under the Panamanian flag for Compania Chilena de Navegacion Interoceanica SA (CCNI). From 1986 until her next sale in 1988 she flew the Chilean flag. Registry then changed to Malta and she was renamed *Agas*. She sailed under her fourth flag, that of the Bahamas, when she was sold to Liberian interests in 1991 and renamed *East Trader*. She flew the Cypriot flag briefly in 1992 before returning to Bahamian registry the same year as *Al Fath*. 1994 saw a further name change to *Cape Vincent* and a return to the Maltese flag. Her seventh and current name was acquired in 1995 when she returned to the Bahamas flag before transferring to Cambodia two years later. Since becoming *Baraka* she has operated for the Egyptian company Romalex Marine.

(Simon Smith)

The "Tourist Ferry" is a popular attraction for visitors to Istanbul. The service starts at Eminönü, the main ferry terminal in Istanbul and proceeds up the Bosphorus crisscrossing the waterway, stopping at various ferry terminals on both the European and Asian sides. Once at the northernmost ferry terminal, Anadolu Kavagı, near the entrance to the Black Sea, the ferry pauses and then makes the return trip. Seen operating the "Tourist Ferry" service and approaching Rumeli Kavagi on 3 June 2008, is the **Büyükada**, a typical Bosphorus ferry. She was built in the Türkiye Gemi Sanayi yard at Kasımpasa, in the Golden Horn, in 1988. In 2010 she was renamed **Karamürsel ALP** and ownership transferred to Kocaeli Büyüksehir Belediyesi, a region of Turkey bordering the Sea of Marmara. Like all the Bosphorus ferries she was originally owned by TDI Sehir Hatları Isletmeleri (TDI City Lines) of Istanbul, part of the state-owned Turkish Maritime Lines. Management of the Istanbul and Bosphorus ferries changed to that of Istanbul Deniz Otobüsleri (IDO) in 2005. For the purposes of this book we will remain at Rumeli Kavagi, a small fishing village on the European shore of the Bosphorus, not far from where the Bosphorus joins the Black Sea. From the hill overlooking the village it is possible to take excellent photographs of the southbound convoy of vessels entering the Bosphorus in the afternoon.

(Chris Brooks)

A real veteran is seen passing Rumeli Kavağı - the Cambodian-flagged *A. Asli*. She was completed in the shipyard of T van Duijvendijk's Scheepswerf at Lekkerkerk in 1959. Originally built for Fearnley & Eger of Norway as the ***Stalheim***, she remained under this name until 1972. Following her sale by Fearnley & Eger she was re-flagged to Panama and renamed ***Mudistar***, a name she retained until 1979. In 1979 she was acquired by the Zar Shipping Co SA of Panama and renamed ***Pardi***, again flagged in Panama. In 1994 she was renamed ***Sonita***, flying the flag of Malta and ownership passed to Sonita Shipping Ltd, of Malta. At this time she was managed by Rota Denizcilik ve Ticaret Ltd Sirketi of Istanbul. She was finally renamed ***A. Asli*** in 1998, and shortly afterwards, transferred to the flag of St Vincent & the Grenadines, though remaining with the same owners and managers. She was again re-flagged by these owners in 2001, this time registered in Phnom Penh and flying the Cambodian flag. In 2008 she was sold to Metmar Mete Denizcilik, of Istanbul, retaining the same name and flag. Sadly her new owners did not keep her long. She arrived off Aliaga in December 2010, her AIS destination poignantly reading "The End of History". At the time of the photograph, taken on 13 August 2009, she was on a voyage from Mariupol, Ukraine, to Mersin, on the Mediterranean coast of Turkey.

(Chris Brooks)

Seen passing Rumeli Kavagi, having just entered the Bosphorus Strait, southbound, from the Black Sea, is the Ukrainian-flagged *Beriks*. Although listed as a general cargo ship, one cannot help but feel, judging by her design, that this vessel had some connection with the fishing industry at one time. Indeed, her owners at the time were registered as Interfish-Biotech Ltd, of Mariupol in the Ukraine. *Beriks* retained her original name from being launched in 1973 at the Yaroslavskiy shipyard, in Yaroslavl, Russia. In recent years she had been a regular caller at Zeytinburnu, a suburb of Istanbul, which has a small port situated in the Sea of Marmara. She traded between that port and ports in the Black Sea. Some details of the trade in which she was involved can be gleaned from reports that in December 2008 she departed from Poti, Georgia, with a cargo of 230 tonnes of frozen meat. This was later spoiled due to the failure of the vessel's refrigeration units. These units were subsequently repaired. However, she remained anchored off the coast of Ukraine with no ports willing to allow her to berth on health grounds. Finally, on 31 July 2009, she was permitted to berth at Odessa. At Odessa repairs were made to the vessel, but the spoiled meat was not offloaded. She finally departed for Turkey on 21 August 2009 with the cargo of rotten meat still on board and arrived at Tuzla on 30 August. From here she departed for Aliaga, arriving there on 19 September. She was broken up at Aliaga during October 2009.

(Chris Brooks)

Making her way into the Black Sea on 5 June 2008 is the Panamanian-flagged bulk carrier **Efstathios**. She was on a voyage from Mersin, Turkey, to Nikolayev in the Ukraine at the time of the photograph. She is owned by the Link Marine Corporation of Panama, but managed by Valiant Shipping SA, based in Greece. She was built in 1988, as the **Lok Pratima** for the Shipping Corporation of India Ltd, by the Garden Reach Shipbuilders & Engineers Ltd of Kolkata. Although launched in 1983 it is interesting to note that she was not completed until 1988. A sistership, **Lok Pragati** was also completed by the same yard in 1984. **Lok Pragati** was broken up at Gadani Beach in March 2009 as the **Suntras**. **Lok Pratima** bore that name up until 2007, when she was sold to her current owners and renamed **Efstathios**. At this time her flag was changed from India to Panama. Prior to the photograph being taken, she was detained at Mersin with a long list of deficiencies. On her next voyage into the Black Sea in November 2008, she arrived at Midia, Romania, for repairs and dry-docking. Whilst at Midia, she suffered a fire in her accommodation on 12 January 2009. The fire delayed the completion of repairs until March 2009.

(Chris Brooks)

The **Geroi Plevny** is a roll-on/roll-off rail vehicles carrier. She is one of a pair of sisterships constructed at Brodogradiliste "Uljanik" at Pula in 1978 for a service between Varna and Illichivsk, her sister being the **Geroi Shipki**. Both vessels were completed for the Black Sea Shipping Co (BLASCO), based in Odessa, Ukraine, flying the flag of the USSR. Ownership was transferred to the ZAO Ukrferry Shipping Co of Odessa in 1999. Since 1993 she has flown the flag of Ukraine. The ferry service between Varna and Illichivsk covers a distance of 426km and takes 17 hours in each direction. Each of the sisterships accommodates 108 twin bogie goods wagons. Fifty passenger berths are also provided. The service was subsequently extended to cover the Georgian ports of Poti and Batumi. Since 2001 frequent calls have also been made to Derince, a Turkish port on the shores of the Sea of Marmara. Photographed passing Rumeli Kavagı on 13 August 2009, the **Geroi Plevny** was on a voyage from Varna to Derince. From her deck cargo it is evident that she is still in use as a rail vehicles carrier.

(Chris Brooks)

One of the older vessels in the Islamic Republic of Iran Shipping Lines (IRISL) fleet is seen passing Rumeli Kavagı southbound on 4 June 2008. The *Iran Modares* had previously departed from Varna, Bulgaria, bound via the Suez Canal for her home port, Bandar Abbas in Iran. *Iran Modares* started life as the *Treana* in 1978, when she was completed at the Kanasashi Shipyard at Toyohashi, Japan, for the Interseas Investment Corporation, based in Greece. She carried this name for only four months, before she was renamed *Gentle River* in April 1978, on her sale to the Lepta Shipping Co Ltd of Liberia. Initially, she changed her flag to that of Liberia, but in December 1978 she was re-flagged to Japan. Her owners from this time were listed as the Hermes Shipping KK, based in Japan. She retained the name *Gentle River* until sold by Hermes Shipping in 1983 to the Islamic Republic of Iran Shipping Lines when she was renamed *Iran Modares*. She was sold to Indian shipbreakers in December 2009 and subsequently beached at Alang in January 2010.

(Chris Brooks)

The *Kurtarma 4* is one of a number of powerful salvage and ship-handling tugs stationed around the Bosphorus. They are normally to be found berthed near the cruise terminal at Istanbul, Haydarpasa, or at their base, near Sarıyer closer to the Black Sea entrance to the Bosphorus. They are primarily used for escorting laden tankers exporting oil from various Black Sea ports through the Bosphorus. Vessels under tow also require an escort tug. The *Kurtarma 4* was launched at the government-owned Izmir Naval Shipyard, at Izmir in 2004 but not completed until mid-2005. She was built for the Kıyı Emniyeti Ve Gemi Kurtarma Isletmeleri Genel Müdürlügü – otherwise known as the Turkish government's General Management of Coastal Safety and Salvage Administration, based in Istanbul. *Kurtarma 4* has an identical sistership, *Kurtarma 3* and also two slightly smaller sisterships, *Kurtarma 1* and *Kurtarma 2*, both completed in 2000 at Izmir. She is seen passing Rumeli Kavagi on 7 October 2008, whilst escorting the laden crude oil tanker *SCF Valdai*, southbound, through the Bosphorus.

(Chris Brooks)

In April 2005 the International Maritime Organisation reached agreement that meant single hull tankers over 30,000 tonnes deadweight would be phased out unless converted to double hull by the time they were twenty-three years old. As the Aframax crude oil tanker **Monte Verde** entered the Bosphorus on 26 June 2006 she had little more than eighteen months trading left. She was launched as the Liberian-flagged **Ionia** by Hitachi Zosen at Innoshima in 1980. A transfer to the Greek flag in 1981 was followed by sale to the French oil company Total. She took the name **Eole** under the French flag. In 1988 she transferred to the Bahamas flag and was renamed **Altus**, continuing to operate for Total. A further sale in 1995 returned her to Greek registry as **Montrose** for Miramar Navigation Corp. By the end of 2004 she was flying the Maltese flag, had been renamed **Monte Verde** and was controlled by London-based tanker operator Seacrest Shipping. Her final sale took place in December 2007 when ownership passed to Pakistani breakers and she was renamed **Shanti**. After passing through the Suez Canal and calling briefly at Jeddah she anchored off Gadani Beach on 13 January 2008. Beaching followed five days later.

(Simon Smith)

Here we see another former British coastal vessel. The livestock carrier **Rihab** started life as general cargo ship **Hyde Park** when she was launched in 1968 at E J Smit & Sons shipyard at Westerbroek, Netherlands. Completed for her owners, Park Steamships Ltd, she was part of the Turnbull Scott group and was a Steamships fleetmate of the **Lisa** also featured in this book. She only remained with this company for four years as she was sold in 1972 and renamed **Philip Lonborg**. In 1974 she became the **Isborg** and 1975 saw her renamed **Sudri** flying the flag of Iceland. She remained under the Icelandic flag for only two years, becoming the Panamanian-flagged **Phoenicia** in 1977. During 1982 she was again sold, this time to Agence Generale Maritime Sarl (AGEMAR) of the Lebanon, renamed **La Palma** and flagged in the Lebanon. In 1991 she was converted from a general cargo ship to a livestock carrier and shortly afterwards, was renamed **Berger A** in 1992. The year 2001 saw her sold to the Barhoum Maritime Co of Tartous, Syria, when she was renamed **Rihab**. Currently she is owned by Rihab Shipping SA of Panama flying the Comoros flag. At the time of the photograph, she had just entered the Bosphorus in the southbound afternoon convoy on 13 August 2009. She was on a voyage from Midia, Romania, to Tartous in Syria.

(Chris Brooks)

Many of the ships illustrated in this volume had completed numerous Bosphorus passages by the time they were photographed. However, on 13 August 2009 the large Greek-flagged bulk carrier **Stella** was entering the narrow channel for the first time. The capesize bulk carrier was on route from her builders, Daewoo-Mangalia Heavy Industries, to load her first cargo at Tubarao. From Tubarao she proceeded across the Pacific Ocean to discharge her cargo, probably iron ore, at the Bao Yuan jetties situated on the Yangtze River just northwest of Shanghai. Daewoo-Mangalia Heavy Industries was established in 1997 as a joint venture between the Korean giant Daewoo and the "2 Maj" Mangalia shipyard situated 45 kilometres south of Constantza. Launched in March 2009, she was listed in official records as **Freeway Pioneer**, but was named **Stella** at a ceremony on 7 August. She is one of two gearless bulk carriers ordered by Tsakos Shipping & Trading S.A. in April 2007 and is the largest bulk carrier constructed to date by a Black Sea shipyard. Sister vessel, yard number 1045, sailed from Mangalia on 14 October 2010 having been named **Ian M** for Tsakos.

(Simon Smith)

The product tanker *Taxiarchis I* commences what proved to be her last Bosphorus transit on 30 May 2008. She was on passage from Odessa for Cyprus with a part cargo. After passing through the Suez Canal in mid-July 2008 she traded in the Middle and Far East before her sale to Pakistani breakers in the autumn of 2009. A product of the Mitsubishi Heavy Industries Nagasaki shipyard, she was launched as *Sweetbrier* in 1985 and delivered to her Liberian flag owners the following year. In 1990 she was sold to Panama flag interests and renamed *President*. Her next change of ownership was in 1998 when she joined the register of Vietnam as *Pacific Falcon* for Falcon Shipping Co Ltd. By 2005 she had returned to the Liberian flag as *Taxiarchis I* for Athens-based owners AK Shipping & Trading Inc as evidenced by her funnel colours. A transfer to the Tuvalu flag and a change of name to *Amsal* in October 2009 was an indication that her days were numbered. In early November she anchored off Gadani Beach and beaching followed on 6 November.

(Simon Smith)